LIFE SKILLS 3
AND
TEST PREP

Howard Pomann   June Pomann

Waldo Cardenas   Raymond Rivera Chabrier

with Jennifer Gaudet

PEARSON

Longman

Life Skills and Test Prep 3

Pearson Education, 10 Bank Street, White Plains, NY 10606

Acknowledgments: The authors wish to acknowledge with gratitude the following reviewers, who helped shape the content and approach of the *Life Skills and Test Prep* series: Dr. Maria H. Koonce, Broward County Schools, Ft. Lauderdale, FL • Dr. G. Santos, The English Center, Miami, FL • Edith Uber, Santa Clara Adult Education, Santa Clara, CA • Merari L. Weber, Metropolitan Skills Center, Glendale Community College, Los Angeles, CA • Theresa Warren, East Side Union High School District, San Jose, CA.

Staff credits: The people who made up the *Life Skills and Test Prep 3* team, representing editorial, production, design, and manufacturing, are Tracey Cataldo, Dave Dickey, Irene Frankel, Melissa Leyva, Wendy Long, Martha McGaughey, and Jane Townsend.

Cover Image: José Ortega c/o theispot.com
Text composition: ElectraGraphics, Inc.
Text font: 11 pt Minion
Illustrations: Steve Attoe: pp. 2, 5, 85, 90, 100 (top right and bottom middle), 105, 110, 132, 142, 143, 144, 148, 158, 162, 164, 185, 197; Gary Torrisi: pp. 55, 64, 65, 66, 67, 73, 79, 86, 87, 88, 96, 100 (bottom right), 120, 121, 122, 124 (bottom), 156, 176, 177.
Technical art: Tinge Design Studio

Library of Congress Cataloging-in-Publication Data
Cardenas, Waldo.
  Life skills and test prep 3 / Waldo Cardenas . . . [et al.].
    p. cm.
Includes bibliographical references.
ISBN 978-0-13-515708-4 (student bk.)—ISBN 978-0-13-515809-8 (audio cd)—ISBN 978-0-13-515808-1 (teacher's manual)
1. English language—Textbooks for foreign speakers. 2. English language—Examinations—Study guides. 3. Life skills—Problems, exercises, etc. I. Title.
  PE1128.C35 2009
  428.2'4—dc22

                        2008030368

ISBN-13: 978-0-13-515708-4
ISBN-10: 0-13-515708-0

PEARSON LONGMAN ON THE **WEB**

Pearsonlongman.com offers online resources for teachers and students. Access our Companion Websites, our online catalog, and our local offices around the world.

Visit us at www.pearsonlongman.com.

Printed in the United States of America

4 2021

Contents

Correlations

Unit 1: Personal Information and Goals	CASAS*	LAUSD**	Florida***
Lesson 1: Giving Personal Information and Work History	0.1.2, 0.1.4, 0.1.5., 0.2.1	1	4.01.01, 4.01.02
Lesson 2: Matching Interests to Possible Jobs	2.8.2, 2.8.3, 2.8.6, 2.8.7, 3.5.7, 4.1.9, 7.1.2, 7.1.4, 7.2.6, 7.2.7, 7.4.2, 7.4.3, 7.4.4, 7.5.1, 7.7.1, 7.7.2, 7.7.3, 7.7.5, 8.3.2	6	4.01.03, 4.03.13
Lesson 3: Setting Goals	0.1.5, 4.1.9, 4.4.5, 7.1.1, 7.1.2, 7.1.3, 7.1.4, 7.2.7	48	4.03.12, 4.03.13
Lesson 4: Interpreting Course Catalogs	0.1.5, 2.5.8, 2.8.1, 2.8.2, 2.8.3, 3.5.7, 4.14, 7.4.4, 7.7.1, 7.7.2, 7.7.3, 7.7.5	13	4.03.05
Lesson 5: Forms and Applications	0.2.2, 2.8.5	2	
Unit 2: Communicating with Others	CASAS	LAUSD	Florida
Lesson 1: Making Casual Conversation	0.1.4, 0.1.8, 0.2.1, 0.2.4, 2.7.2, 2.7.3, 2.7.7, 2.7.8, 2.7.9, 7.5.6	3	4.01.01, 4.01.02, 4.01.04
Lesson 2: Giving and Responding to Compliments	0.1.4, 0.1.5, 0.2.1, 0.2.4, 7.2.2, 7.2.5, 7.5.6	4c	4.01.01, 4.01.02, 4.01.04
Lesson 3: Making and Responding to Apologies	4c	4b	4.01.04
Lesson 4: Thank-You Notes	0.2.3, 7.5.6	9	4.01.01

*CASAS: Comprehensive Adult Student Assessment Systems Competency List,
**LAUSD: Los Angeles Unified School District (ESL Intermediate Low content standards)
***Florida: Adult ESOL Low Intermediate standardized syllabi

Unit 3: The American School System	CASAS	LAUSD	Florida
Lesson 1: American School Structure	2.8.1	10	4.02.07
Lesson 2: Report Cards	0.1.5, 0.2.4, 2.8.4, 2.8.8	10, 57	4.02.07

Unit 4: Talking on the Phone	CASAS	LAUSD	Florida
Lesson 1: Calling Directory Assistance	0.1.2, 0.1.7, 2.1.1	14	4.01.06
Lesson 2: Taking and Receiving Messages	0.1.6, 0.1.7, 2.1.7, 2.1.8	17	4.01.06, 4.01.07
Lesson 3: Leaving Messages on Answering Machines and Voice Mail	0.1.5, 2.1.7, 2.1.8	18	4.01.07
Lesson 4: Using Automated Phone Systems	0.1.5, 1.2.6, 1.3.1, 1.3.6	19	4.04.02, 4.04.09

Unit 5: Community Information	CASAS	LAUSD	Florida
Lesson 1: Giving and Getting Directions	0.1.5, 0.1.6, 0.1.7, 1.1.3, 1.9.4, 2.2.1, 2.2.5, 6.6.5, 7.4.8	7a, 20	4.06.03
Lesson 2: Library Services	2.5.6, 7.4.4, 7.7.1, 7.7.2, 7.7.3, 7.7.5	21	4.02.02
Lesson 3: Preparing for an Emergency	0.1.5, 3.4.3, 3.4.8, 7.4.5		4.02.05

Unit 6: Transportation	CASAS	LAUSD	Florida
Lesson 1: Transportation Schedules	0.1.5, 2.2.1, 2.2.3, 2.2.4, 2.5.1	22	4.06.01
Lesson 2: Transportation Announcements	2.2.4, 7.4.5	22	4.06.01
Lesson 3: Parts of a Car	0.1.5, 1.7.3, 1.9.2, 1.9.9	23	
Lesson 4: Car Maintenance	0.1.5, 1.7.4, 1.9.6	23	4.06.05
Lesson 5: After a Car Accident	0.1.5, 1.7.5, 1.9.7, 1.9.8	34	4.06.04

Unit 7: Money and Housing	CASAS	LAUSD	Florida
Lesson 1: Bank Accounts	0.1.5, 1.8.1, 1.8.2, 1.8.3, 6.0.1	25c	4.04.07
Lesson 2: Credit Cards	0.1.5, 1.5.3, 1.8.1, 1.8.2, 1.8.3, 1.8.4, 1.8.6, 6.0.1	25d, 27	4.01.08, 4.04.02
Lesson 3: Looking for an Apartment or a House	0.1.5, 1.4.1, 1.4.2, 6.0.1	26	4.04.04
Lesson 4: Rental Agreements	0.1.5, 1.4.3, 1.4.4, 1.4.5, 7.4.5	26	
Unit 8: Food and Shopping	CASAS	LAUSD	Florida
Lesson 1: Following Recipes	0.1.5, 1.1.1, 1.1.7, 1.2.8, 1.3.8, 6.0.2, 8.2.1	31	
Lesson 2: Interpreting Coupons and Ads	1.1.6, 1.1.8, 1.2.1, 1.2.3, 1.2.5, 1.2.9, 1.3.9, 1.6.5, 6.0.2, 6.0.3, 6.0.4, 6.0.5, 6.2.2, 6.2.3, 6.2.5, 6.2.6, 6.4.1, 6.4.3, 6.4.4, 6.4.5	29	4.04.01, 4.04.03, 4.04.06
Lesson 3: Comparison Shopping	0.1.5, 1.1.6, 1.2.5	28, 49	4.04.01, 4.04.03
Lesson 4: Making Returns	0.1.5, 1.3.3, 1.6.3, 7.3.1, 7.3.2, 7.3.3, 7.3.4, 7.4.5	30	
Lesson 5: Understanding Warranties	0.1.5, 1.7.1, 7.3.1, 7.3.2, 7.3.4		
Unit 9: Holidays, Government, and Law	CASAS	LAUSD	Florida
Lesson 1: Holidays in the United States	2.7.1	33	4.02.03
Lesson 2: The U.S. Government	0.1.5, 5.5.2, 5.5.3, 5.5.4, 5.5.9	32	
Lesson 3: Reporting a Crime	2.5.1, 5.3.5, 5.3.7, 5.3.8, 5.5.6	35	4.07.02

Unit 10: Health	CASAS	LAUSD	Florida
Lesson 1: Parts of the Body	3.1.1, 3.6.1	36	
Lesson 2: Diseases and Medical Conditions	0.1.5, 1.1.5, 3.1.1, 3.6.2, 3.6.3	38	4.05.01
Lesson 3: Medical History Forms	0.2.2, 3.2.1	41	
Lesson 4: Symptoms	1.1.5, 3.1.1, 3.4.7, 3.6.3	37	4.05.01
Lesson 5: Immunization Requirements	2.5.3, 3.1.3, 3.2.2, 3.4.6, 3.5.9	39	4.05.05
Lesson 6: Good Health	0.1.5, 1.2.8, 1.3.8, 3.4.2, 3.4.5, 3.5.1, 3.5.2, 3.5.4, 3.5.5, 3.5.8, 3.5.9, 3.5.7, 3.6.5, 8.1.1		4.05.02, 4.05.06, 4.07.01
Unit 11: Getting a Job	CASAS	LAUSD	Florida
Lesson 1: Looking for a Job	0.1.5, 4.1.3, 7.4.4, 7.7.1, 7.7.2, 7.7.3, 7.7.5	53	
Lesson 2: Applying for Jobs	0.1.5, 4.1.2, 4.1.8, 4.1.9	42	4.03.01, 4.03.02
Lesson 3: Job Applications	0.1.5, 0.2.2, 4.1.2, 4.1.6	45	4.03.01, 4.03.02
Lesson 4: Job Interviews	0.1.1, 0.1.5, 4.1.4, 4.1.5, 4.1.7	43, 44	4.01.04, 4.03.04
Unit 12: At Work	CASAS	LAUSD	Florida
Lesson 1: Work Schedules	2.3.2, 2.3.4, 4.1.6		
Lesson 2: Communicating at Work	4.4.6, 4.6.1, 4.8.1, 4.8.2, 4.8.5, 4.8.6, 4.8.7, 4.9.3	47	4.03.07, 4.03.09, 4.03.10
Lesson 3: Pay Day	4.2.1		

To the Teacher

Course Overview

Life Skills and Test Prep 3 is a competency-based, four-skills course for adult ESL students at the low-intermediate level. It is designed to help students acquire the language and life skills competencies they need in all their roles—at home, at work, in school, and in their communities. The course also includes listening and reading tests to give students invaluable practice in taking standardized tests, motivating them to achieve their benchmarks and persist in their learning goals.

Unit Organization

There are twelve units, organized thematically. Each unit contains from three to six lessons, each one focusing on a specific competency, such as reading an ad for an apartment, completing a job application, or taking a phone message. The first page of the unit lists the lessons in the unit, along with the goal(s) for each lesson.

At the end of each unit, there is a unit test with both a listening and a reading section. This unit test is a multiple-choice test, much like the CASAS test or other standardized tests. Students must bubble in their answers on a separate answer sheet, found in the back of the book. The answer sheet is perforated so students can easily remove it.

Lesson Organization

Lessons are composed of the following elements as appropriate for the competency being presented:

- Learn
- Practice
- Make It Yours
- Listen
- Note
- Bonus

Note: Listening activities occur throughout the lesson. The icon before the direction line indicates the CD number and track.

Learn

Each lesson begins with a section called Learn, where the target competency is introduced. Some competencies focus on speaking and listening, while others focus on reading and writing. However, all four skills are integrated within the lesson.

Practice

In the Practice section, students apply what they have just learned. Practice exercises vary in type, depending on the competency. Practice sections often present model conversations, such as someone calling about renting an apartment. Here are the steps for most model conversations:

1. Students first listen to the conversation.
2. They practice the conversation in pairs.
3. They reverse roles and practice the conversation again.
4. They practice the conversation again, substituting other information provided.

Make It Yours

This section allows students to personalize the material. These activities range from controlled role plays to more open-ended discussions.

Listen

In addition to the listening exercises built into the other sections of the lesson, every unit includes at least one Listen section that focuses on listening discrimination. The Listen section further reinforces the material in the lesson.

Note

Notes on language and culture appear in the lesson as needed. Additional notes give practical information related to the life skill competency. For example, a note in a lesson about report cards explains the grading system A–F used in most U.S. schools.

Bonus

The Bonus section that occurs at the end of lessons presents optional activities that go beyond the competency, giving students additional speaking and writing practice.

Unit Tests

Unit tests appear after every unit and contain both a listening and a reading section.

Listening

The listening section includes a variety of item types and is divided into two or three parts.

In the first, and sometimes second, part, students listen to the questions but read the answer choices on the test page. The directions for this section are as follows:

- Listen to the sentence. Which of the following means the same as the sentence you heard: A, B, or C?
- Listen to the first part of the conversation. What should the person say next: A, B, or C?
- You will hear a conversation. Then you will hear a question about the conversation. What is the correct answer: A, B, or C?

In the last part, everything—all questions and answers—is on the audio CD. The answer choices are *not* on the test page. The directions for this section are as follows:

- Listen. Everything is on the audio CD. Listen to the question and three answers. What is the correct answer: A, B, or C?

Each question in the listening sections is on a separate track on the audio CD. We recommend that you *play each track twice*, pausing for 10 to 20 seconds between each play. This will approximate how listening is presented on standardized tests.

Reading

The reading section tests students' ability to read and answer questions about a variety of print material, such as signs, forms, schedules, and paragraphs.

Answer Sheets

Each unit test is formatted like a standardized test. Students fill in (bubble in) their answers on the perforated answer sheets included in the back of the book. The answer sheets are printed on both sides of the page in case you want the students to take a test twice or to have additional practice completing the required personal information.

Answer Keys

The answer keys and audioscripts for the tests are found in the *Life Skills and Test Prep 3 Teacher's Manual*. Each answer key can be used as a scoring mask to make tests easy to grade. It also serves as a diagnostic tool; each test item is labeled with its corresponding objective, giving you a clear picture of which competencies the student has not yet acquired.

Life Skills and Test Prep 3 Teacher's Manual

In addition to the answer keys described above, the *Life Skills and Test Prep 3 Teacher's Manual* includes a section to prepare students for the tests in the book and for standardized tests. It helps students use an answer sheet, understand the directions in a test, and learn important test-taking strategies. We recommend that you go through this section of the manual with students before they take the Unit 1 Test or before they take the post-test on a standardized test.

The manual also includes a Classroom Methodology section, with general information for using the *Life Skills and Test Prep 3* material. This section suggests ways for doing pair and group work activities, presenting vocabulary, checking answers, and correcting students' language production.

Please ask your Pearson Longman rep about this manual if you do not already have it.

Built-in Flexibility

Life Skills and Test Prep 3 provides 80 to 100 hours of class instruction. All the material in is aimed at low-intermediate students. As such, the lessons do not have to be taught in a specific order, and lessons may be skipped. If you do not want to use all the lessons, here are some ideas for how to select which ones to use:

- Ask your students which topics they are interested in and teach only those lessons.
- Give the unit test as a pre-test to find out how students perform. Use the diagnostic information in the *Life Skills and Test Prep 3 Teacher's Manual* to guide you to which lessons students need.
- If you are using *Life Skills and Test Prep 3* along with *Center Stage 3*, use the information in the *Center Stage 3 Teacher's Edition* to direct you to specific lessons.

To the Student

Life Skills and Test Prep 3 will help you improve your scores on ESL tests like the CASAS test. It will help you prepare for these tests in several ways:

- You will learn the English skills you need for the test.

- You will learn about tests and test-taking strategies.

- You will take a test after each unit, which will give you practice in taking tests and using answer sheets.

Preparing to Take a Test

Here are some things you can do to prepare for a test.

☐ Get a lot of sleep the night before the test.

☐ Eat a meal or snack before the test.

☐ Bring two sharpened #2 pencils.

☐ Bring a pencil eraser.

☐ Bring a ruler or a blank piece of paper.

☐ Arrive early at the testing room.

☐ Make sure you can easily see and hear the tester.

☐ Turn off your cell phone.

☐ Try to relax and do your best! Good luck!

Unit 1

Personal Information and Goals

Learn

Read the story. Then complete each sentence. Circle the correct word or phrase.

Carlos Reyes is from Lima, Peru. Carlos grew up and graduated from high school in Lima. After high school, he studied business at a university in Lima for two years. He left the university before he graduated because he needed to work full-time. Carlos got a job as a travel agent.

Carlos came to the United States in 2006. When he arrived, he lived in Washington, D.C. After his first year, Carlos moved to Baltimore, Maryland, where he still lives now. Carlos has never married, and he doesn't have any children. His family still lives in Peru, so he shares an apartment in Baltimore with a roommate. Carlos is very busy, and his life is not easy. He works forty hours a week at a men's clothing store, and he is also studying English three nights a week at the local high school. Carlos has been taking classes to improve his English so he can go back to college and finish his degree. After he graduates, he wants to get a job in sales or marketing.

1. Carlos is a **high school** / **college** graduate.
2. In Peru, Carlos studied **English / business**.
3. When he lived in Peru, Carlos worked for a **university / travel agency**.
4. Carlos lived in **Washington, D.C. / Baltimore, Maryland** for a year.
5. Carlos is **single / married**.
6. Carlos works at a **store / local high school**.
7. Carlos **is already taking / wants to start taking** English classes.
8. Carlos wants to **work at a college / get his college degree**.

Practice

A ◎ 6 **Carlos is talking to an admissions adviser at Sunset Community College. Listen and read the conversation. Then practice with a partner.**

A: Hi, <u>Carlos</u>. I'm Mike Torres.
B: Hi, Mike, nice to meet you.
A: <u>Carlos</u>, tell me about yourself. Where are you from?
B: <u>Lima, Peru</u>.
A: OK. Tell me about your education.
B: Well, I <u>graduated from high school in Lima. And then I studied business at a university there for two years</u>.
A: I see. So what did you do after that?
B: <u>I worked as a travel agent</u>.
A: And when did you come to the United States?
B: <u>Three years ago</u>.
A: Uh-huh. And what are you doing now?
B: <u>I'm working as a salesperson at a men's clothing store. I've also been studying English at night</u>.

B *PAIRS.* **Read the information about each person. Then complete the chart.**

> Yao Ling is from Shanghai, China. He grew up and finished high school in Shanghai. Then he studied engineering for four years at Shanghai University. After graduation he worked for Wesley, a U.S. computer company, for two years. He came to the United States last year. Right now he has a job at Big Electric, an electronics store.

> Tansu Biret is from Istanbul, Turkey. She grew up and finished high school in Istanbul. After high school she got a job working as a receptionist at an international hotel. She came to the United States four years ago. Now she's working at Hotel Mark. She's a receptionist. Last year she started taking English classes two days a week.

	Yao Ling	Tansu Biret
Where is the person from?		
What is the person's educational background?		
What is the person's work experience?		
When did the person come to the United States?		
What is the person doing now?		

C *PAIRS. ROLE PLAY.* **Read the information about the people in Exercise B on page 3 again. Use the information to make new conversations like the one in Exercise A. Switch roles.**

Listen

 Listen to the questions. What is the correct answer? Circle *a, b,* **or** *c.*

1. **a.** two years ago   **b.** Mexico   **c.** high school

2. **a.** Yes, I did.   **b.** No, I started university.   **c.** Yes, I started school in 2005.

3. **a.** I graduated last year.   **b.** I work at a supermarket.   **c.** in New York

4. **a.** Bogotá, Colombia   **b.** Yes, I want to go to school.   **c.** I studied for two years.

5. **a.** for two years   **b.** three nights a week   **c.** four years ago

6. **a.** English   **b.** at a university in my country   **c.** a travel agent

Make It Yours

A **Make notes on your own personal information and work history. Answer the questions.**

Where are you from?

What is your educational background?

What jobs have you had in the past?

When did you come to the United States?

What do you do now?

B *PAIRS. ROLE PLAY.* **Practice the conversation on page 3 again. Use your own or made-up information. Switch roles.**

BONUS   *CLASS.* **Introduce your partner from Make It Yours, Exercise B. Tell the class two things you learned about your partner.**

Matching Interests to Possible Jobs

Learn

A CD1 TRACK 8 and 9 **Look at the pictures. Listen to people's likes and abilities. Listen and repeat.**

1. I enjoy working as part of a group.

2. I enjoy working independently.

3. I enjoy taking care of people.

4. I'm a good listener, and I enjoy helping people.

5. I enjoy organizing things.

6. I enjoy working with my hands.

7. I enjoy supervising people.

8. I'm friendly and outgoing.

9. I have strong problem-solving skills.

Learn

A   Read the story.

> Lara came to the United States from Russia four years ago. She is taking an intermediate English class at night. During the day, she works as a receptionist. She would like a different job, but she's not sure what career she wants. Lara went to a career counselor at her school for advice. The counselor suggested that Lara fill out an interests survey.

B   Read Lara's interests survey.

	YES	SOMETIMES	NO
1. I enjoy taking care of people.	✓		
2. I enjoy working in an office.		✓	
3. I enjoy painting, drawing, and taking photographs.	✓		
4. I enjoy organizing things.	✓		
5. I enjoy teaching people how to do things.	✓		
6. I enjoy supervising people.	✓		
7. I prefer working outside.			✓
8. I enjoy working as part of a group.	✓		
9. I enjoy working independently.			✓
10. I enjoy working with children.		✓	
11. I enjoy selling things.			✓
12. I'm good at fixing things.			✓
13. I want to make a lot of money.		✓	
14. I have strong science and math skills.		✓	
15. I like to have clear directions and rules when I'm working.		✓	
16. I have strong problem-solving skills.	✓		
17. I'm a good listener, and I enjoy helping people.	✓		
18. I'm friendly and outgoing.	✓		
19. I'm good at getting other people to agree with me.		✓	
20. I enjoy doing something different every day.		✓	
21. I enjoy working with my hands.			✓
22. I'm good with numbers.		✓	

Practice

A   **Look at Lara's interests survey again. Write the sentences from the survey that have similar meanings to the sentences below.**

1. I like to work alone.

   I enjoy working independently.
   _____

2. I'm good at science and math.

   _____

3. I like to make friends and meet new people.

   _____

4. I like to work with other people.

   _____

5. I like to do things with my hands.

   _____

6. I'm good at changing people's opinions to my opinion.

   _____

7. I'm good at finding solutions to problems.

   _____

8. I like to listen to people's problems, and I like to help them.

   _____

B   **Look at Lara's interests survey again. Read the sentences. Circle *T* for True or *F* for False.**

1. Lara wants to work outside.	T (F)
2. For Lara, it's better to work with a group of people than alone.	T F
3. Lara is good at solving problems.	T F
4. Lara likes to help people.	T F
5. Lara likes to meet new people.	T F
6. Lara likes making things and fixing things with her hands.	T F

C   *PAIRS.* **Ask each other questions about the results of Lara's interests survey. Take turns.**

> *Example:*
>
> *A: Does Lara enjoy taking care of people?*
> *B: Yes, she does. But she doesn't like working outside.*

Make It Yours

A   **Complete the survey below about your own interests. Read each sentence and check the answer that is true for you.**

	YES	SOMETIMES	NO
1. I enjoy taking care of people.			
2. I enjoy working in an office.			
3. I enjoy painting, drawing, and taking photographs.			
4. I enjoy organizing things.			
5. I enjoy teaching people how to do things.			
6. I enjoy supervising people.			
7. I prefer working outside.			
8. I enjoy working as part of a group.			
9. I enjoy working independently.			
10. I enjoy working with children.			
11. I enjoy selling things.			
12. I'm good at fixing things.			
13. I want to make a lot of money.			
14. I have strong science and math skills.			
15. I like to have clear directions and rules when I'm working.			
16. I have strong problem-solving skills.			
17. I'm a good listener, and I enjoy helping people.			
18. I'm friendly and outgoing.			
19. I'm good at getting other people to agree with me.			
20. I enjoy doing something different every day.			
21. I enjoy working with my hands.			
22. I'm good with numbers.			

B   *PAIRS.* **Ask each other questions about your interests surveys.**

Example:

A: Do you enjoy taking care of people?
B: No, I don't, but I like painting, drawing, and taking photographs.

Learn

A   **Read the story.**

> After Lara completed her interests survey, she found two jobs that matched her interests and skills: medical assistant and licensed practical nurse. She went online and learned about the requirements for those jobs, including the education needed. She learned about the responsibilities and work schedules of both jobs and how much the jobs paid. Her counselor said to use that information to list the advantages and disadvantages of each position, according to her own likes and dislikes.

B   **Read Lara's lists of advantages and disadvantages for the careers of medical assistant and licensed practical nurse.**

Medical Assistant (MA)

Advantages	Disadvantages
• less education needed	• will probably make less money
• often work in doctors' office so probably no holiday, night, or weekend work	• do more office work; MAs don't give as much direct patient care
• might be easier to find MA job than LPN job in future	• must work under supervision of doctor, nurse, or office manager

Licensed Practical Nurse (LPN)

Advantages	Disadvantages
• will probably make more money	• more education needed
• work directly with patients	• long hours, often have to work holidays, nights, and weekends
• can sometimes work independently, without doctor's supervision	
• can more easily become higher-level nurse, such as registered nurse, in future	

Practice

Look at Lara's lists on page 9 again. Read the sentences. Circle *T* for True or *F* for False.

1. The lists show good and bad things about each job.   (T) F
2. Lara wants to provide care directly to patients.   T   F
3. She doesn't want to work at night or on weekends.   T   F
4. Lara thinks there will be more LPN jobs than MA jobs in the future.   T   F
5. Lara always likes to work under direct supervision.   T   F
6. She might want to become a registered nurse in the future.   T   F

BONUS

A Choose two jobs that might interest you based on the results of your interests survey on page 8. You can look at library materials or go online to the Federal Occupational Handbook (www.bls.gov) for ideas. Find out the requirements for each job, including the education you need. Find out the responsibilities and work schedules of the jobs and how much each job pays. Then write lists of the advantages and disadvantages of each position, like the ones on page 9.

B *PAIRS.* Talk about these jobs with a partner. Based on your lists of advantages and disadvantages, is there a job you think you want?

Lesson 3 Setting Goals

Learn

Note A goal is something you hope to do or to achieve in the future. When you set a goal, you have to think about how and when you will reach it. You need to plan the steps to take. The first steps you need to take become your short-term goals. The next steps are mid-term goals. After completing those steps, you are ready to work on reaching your long-term goal.

A **Read the story.**

Arcelia Rodriguez was a child-care worker in Monterrey, Mexico. After she moved to the United States, she got a job as an assistant in a day care center. She's been working there since then. Her long-term goal is to become a teacher for preschool students (ages 2–5). She knows she needs an associate (two-year) degree in early childhood education to get a preschool teaching job in her area. She also knows she has to improve her English to study for the degree. Arcelia has made a chart of her short-term, mid-term, and long-term goals, including how and when she plans to reach each of them.

B **CD1 TRACK 10 Look at Arcelia's chart of her short-term, mid-term, and long-term goals. Listen and read.**

	HOW WILL I ACHIEVE THE GOAL?	WHEN WILL I ACHIEVE THE GOAL?
SHORT-TERM GOAL • improve English skills to prepare for college courses	• take intermediate ESL course at Vista Adult School	• finish semester by May 2010
MID-TERM GOALS • get accepted to Freemont Community College • get associate degree in early childhood education at FCC	• complete application • take two classes a semester	• send application by June 2010 • get degree in May 2013
LONG-TERM GOAL • get job as preschool teacher	• learn and practice good interview skills	• find a job by December 2013

Practice

PAIRS. **Read Arcelia's story and look at the chart of her goals on page 11 again. Answer the questions.**

1. What is Arcelia's job now? _____

2. What job does she want to have? _____

3. What is her short-term goal? _____

4. How does Arcelia plan to improve her English? _____

5. What are her mid-term goals? _____

6. When does she want to finish her degree? _____

7. What is she going to learn after she finishes her degree? _____

8. When does Aracelia want to achieve her long-term goal? _____

Listen

11 **Listen to different students talk about their goals. Answer the questions. Circle *a*, *b*, or *c*.**

1. What is Lucy's long-term goal?

   a. to be a teaching assistant   **b.** to be a teacher   **c.** to be a student

2. What does Javier want to study in the future?

   a. English   **b.** education   **c.** business

3. What is Nina going to do first after she finishes her English class?

   a. look for a job   **b.** work at the same job   **c.** take classes at the community college

4. What is the man's short-term goal?

   a. to find a part-time job   **b.** to finish college   **c.** to take an ESL class

Make It Yours

A Think about a job you would like to have. (It might be a job you described in the Bonus section on page 10. Or use your imagination!) Let that job be your long-term goal. What steps do you need to take to get the job? Make those your short- and mid-term goals. Fill in the chart below.

	How will I achieve the goal?	When will I achieve the goal?
Short-term goals		
Mid-term goals		
Long-term goals		

B Look at your chart again. Ask yourself the following questions:

Have I thought about all the steps?

Do I need to set any smaller goals before I can achieve my main goals?

Do I need to do any more research?

Have I thought about how to reach my goals?

Have I set dates for achieving them?

Have I given myself enough time to complete each goal?

C *PAIRS.* Share your chart with a partner. Talk about your goals. Help each other think about the questions above.

BONUS *CLASS.* Share your future goals with the class. Explain what you will do to achieve each goal and when you will do it.

Lesson 4 Interpreting Course Catalogs

Learn

Note Adult education classes can prepare students for the citizenship test, the GED test (General Equivalency Diplomacy or General Educational Development), or specific jobs. They are often taught at local high schools, community centers, learning centers, or community colleges.

A Look at the online catalog of courses at an adult education center.

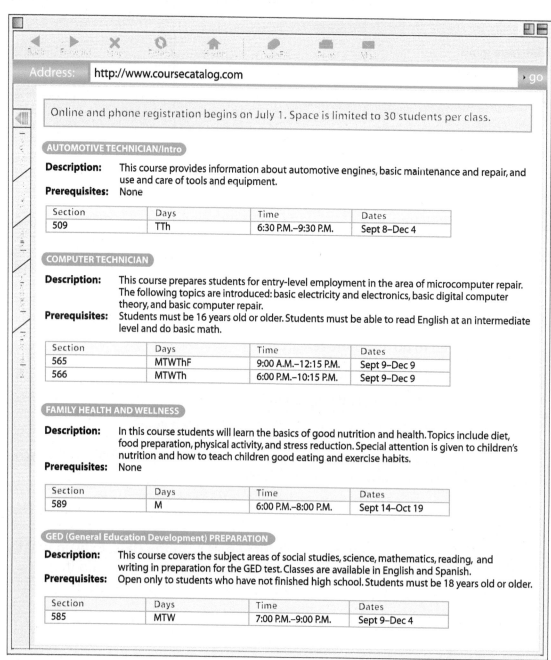

Address: http://www.coursecatalog.com › go

Online and phone registration begins on July 1. Space is limited to 30 students per class.

AUTOMOTIVE TECHNICIAN/Intro

Description: This course provides information about automotive engines, basic maintenance and repair, and use and care of tools and equipment.
Prerequisites: None

Section	Days	Time	Dates
509	TTh	6:30 P.M.–9:30 P.M.	Sept 8–Dec 4

COMPUTER TECHNICIAN

Description: This course prepares students for entry-level employment in the area of microcomputer repair. The following topics are introduced: basic electricity and electronics, basic digital computer theory, and basic computer repair.
Prerequisites: Students must be 16 years old or older. Students must be able to read English at an intermediate level and do basic math.

Section	Days	Time	Dates
565	MTWThF	9:00 A.M.–12:15 P.M.	Sept 9–Dec 9
566	MTWTh	6:00 P.M.–10:15 P.M.	Sept 9–Dec 9

FAMILY HEALTH AND WELLNESS

Description: In this course students will learn the basics of good nutrition and health. Topics include diet, food preparation, physical activity, and stress reduction. Special attention is given to children's nutrition and how to teach children good eating and exercise habits.
Prerequisites: None

Section	Days	Time	Dates
589	M	6:00 P.M.–8:00 P.M.	Sept 14–Oct 19

GED (General Education Development) PREPARATION

Description: This course covers the subject areas of social studies, science, mathematics, reading, and writing in preparation for the GED test. Classes are available in English and Spanish.
Prerequisites: Open only to students who have not finished high school. Students must be 18 years old or older.

Section	Days	Time	Dates
585	MTW	7:00 P.M.–9:00 P.M.	Sept 9–Dec 4

B   Look at the catalog again. Match the words with their definitions.

_____ 1. catalog

_____ 2. technician

_____ 3. basic

_____ 4. maintenance

_____ 5. prerequisite

_____ 6. section

_____ 7. entry-level
     employment

a. skilled scientific or industrial worker

b. condition that must be met before you can do
   something

c. number of a specific class

d. a beginning job

e. complete list of things you can buy, classes you can
   take, etc.

f. work that is necessary to keep something in good
   condition

g. beginning level

C   Look at the catalog again. Answer the questions.

1. Is it important to register early? Why? _____

2. How many days a week is the automotive technician course? _____

3. What are the prerequisites for the computer technician course? _____

4. What day does the family health and wellness course begin? _____

5. What languages are the GED courses available in? _____

6. Which course prepares students for a job? _____

Listen

12 Listen to the conversations. Answer the questions. Circle *a*, *b*, or *c*.

1. What course is the man interested in?

   a. computer technician   **b.** computer programmer   **c.** automotive technician

2. What times does the course meet?

   a. 6:00 to 9:00 P.M.   **b.** 7:00 to 9:00 P.M.   **c.** 7:00 to 8:30 P.M.

3. How long does the course last?

   a. 12 weeks   **b.** 16 weeks   **c.** 19 weeks

4. What day does the class meet?

   a. Monday   **b.** Saturday   **c.** Sunday

Practice

A **13** Look at the brochure for an adult education center and listen to the conversation. Then practice with a partner.

CIN 824 Intro to Auto Mechanics 5:30 P.M. 8:30 P.M. T TH $350 16 weeks	**CIN 624 Basic Computer Skills** 7:00 P.M. 9:00 P.M. T TH $175 12 weeks
CIN 345 Administrative Assistant Basics 6:30 P.M. 8:30 P.M. M W $250 16 weeks	**CIN 132 Citizenship** 7:00 P.M. 9:00 P.M. W Free 12 weeks
CIN 425 Health and Nutrition 5:30 P.M. 9:30 P.M. M T W $150 16 weeks	**CIN 154 Beginning ESOL** 7:00 P.M. 9:00 P.M. T TH Free 20 weeks
CIN 286 Intro to Child Care 6:30 P.M. 8:30 P.M. M T $150 12 weeks	

A: Hello. Indigo Adult School.
B: Hello. I'm interested in your <u>Intro to Auto Mechanics</u> class. When does the class meet?
A: It meets from <u>5:30 to 8:30 on Tuesdays and Thursdays</u>.
B: OK. And how much does the course cost?
A: <u>$350.</u>
B: And how long does it last?
A: <u>16 weeks</u>.
B: Can I register over the phone?
A: Yes. You can call 415-555-2632 or you can register online.
B: OK. Thank you.
A: You're welcome.

B *PAIRS. ROLE PLAY.* Practice the conversation. Use the information about the different courses in the adult education brochure.

Make It Yours

A *GROUPS OF 3.* What courses have you taken or are you taking now? Where were/are the classes? Was/Is there a fee? What did/do you learn in the class?

> **BONUS** *GROUPS OF 3.* Bring in brochures from your school and other schools in your area. Make a list of the courses that are interesting to you. How often do the classes meet? How long are they? How much do they cost?

Lesson 5 Forms and Applications

Learn

A   Read Carlos's application for Sunset Community College.

Sunset Community College Application Form

PERSONAL INFORMATION

Last Name: Reyes   First Name: Carlos

Address: 32 Watson Street, Santa Ana, TX 33001

Home Phone: 737-555-1037   Email Address: creyes@gmail.com

This section is voluntary. The information is requested for local, state and federal reporting purposes only. It will not be used for consideration in admission.

Race Ethnicity: (Check all that apply.)

   ☐ African American Black   ☐ American Indian or Alaska Native   ☐ Other

   ☐ Asian   ☐ Pacific Islander

   ☐ White   ✓ Hispanic

Sex: Male

Are you a United States veteran?   No

Did one or both of your parents attend college?   No

CITIZENSHIP INFORMATION

Are you a U.S. citizen?   No   If no, what is your country of citizenship?   Peru

Type of Visa: (Check one.)   ✓ Permanent Resident   ☐ Student (F-1)   ☐ Other

EDUCATIONAL INFORMATION

Have you either graduated from high school or received a GED?   Yes

If yes, when?   June 2010

Name of school: Central High School

Address of school: 24 Washington Blvd, Santa Ana, Texas, Peru

Have you attended any other colleges, universities, or vocational technical schools?   Yes

If yes, when?   July 2012   to   June 2013   Did you graduate?   No

Name of school: Hudson Adult School

Address of school: 180 Lewis Blvd, Jefferson, Washington, Texas 33, Peru

When do you want to begin studying at Sunset Community College? (Check one.)

   ☐ spring semester   ✓ fall semester   ☐ summer session   year   2020

Do you want to study full time or part time?   part time

Why do you want to **enroll** at Sunset Community College? (Check all that apply.)

   ☐ Personal Interest   ✓ Improve skills to get a job, new job, promotion

   ☐ Improve skills for current job   ☐ Transfer to another college university

   ✓ Earn a two year degree   ☐ Earn a certificate (non degree)

   ☐ Unknown ☐ Other

I certify that all information given on this application is true.

Signature: Carlos Reyes   Date: July 2020

B Read Carlos's application on page 17 again. Match the words with their definitions.

__g__ 1. voluntary

_____ 2. veteran

_____ 3. attend

_____ 4. semester

_____ 5. full-time

_____ 6. part-time

_____ 7. enroll

_____ 8. transfer

a. someone who has served in the military

b. leave one school and register at another

c. half a school year (usually 12–16 weeks at a college)

d. studying or working less than a regular schedule

e. register or sign up for classes

f. studying or working a regular, full schedule

g. optional, not required

h. go to school, a class, etc.

Practice

Read Carlos's application on page 17 again. Then read the sentences below. Circle *T* for *True* or *F* for *False*.

1. Carlos is a student at Sunset Community College. **T** (**F**)

2. Carlos lives in Peru. **T** **F**

3. Carlos left his university in 2004. **T** **F**

4. Carlos doesn't have to give information about his race or ethnicity. **T** **F**

5. Carlos will have a better chance of being accepted by the college if he fills out the demographic information. **T** **F**

6. Carlos has served in the U.S. military. **T** **F**

7. Carlos graduated from the Colegio Santa Ana. **T** **F**

8. Carlos's reason for studying at Sunset Community College is to get a diploma. **T** **F**

9. Carlos wants to enroll at Sunset Community College. **T** **F**

10. Carlos has given only true information on the form. **T** **F**

Make It Yours

Complete the application for a community college. Use your own or made-up information.

Valley Community College Application Form

PERSONAL INFORMATION

Last Name: First Name:

Address:

Home Phone: Email Address:

This section is voluntary. The information is requested for local, state, and federal reporting purposes only. It will not be used for consideration in admission.

Race/Ethnicity: (Check all that apply.)

    African American/Black   American Indian or Alaska Native   Other

    Asian   Pacific Islander

    White   Hispanic

Sex:

Are you a United States veteran?

Did one or both of your parents attend college?

CITIZENSHIP INFORMATION

Are you a U.S. citizen?   If no, what is your country of citizenship?

Type of Visa: (Check one.)   Permanent Resident   Student (F 1)   Other

EDUCATIONAL INFORMATION

Have you either graduated from high school or received a GED?

If yes, when?

Name of school:

Address of school:

Have you attended any other colleges, universities, or vocational technical schools?

If yes, when?   to   Did you graduate?

Name of school:

Address of school:

When do you want to begin studying at Valley Community College? (Check one.)

    spring semester   fall semester   summer session   year

Do you want to study full time or part time?

Why do you want to enroll at Valley Community College? (Check all that apply.)

    Personal interest   Improve skills to get a job / new job / promotion

    Improve skills for current job   Transfer to another college/university

    Earn a two year degree   Earn a certificate (non degree)

    Unknown / Other

I certify that all information given on this application is true.

Signature: Date:

Unit 1 Test

Listening I [Tracks 14–17]

Listen to the first part of the conversation. What should the person say next: A, B, or C?

1. A. I got my GED.

   B. I'm working as a travel agent.

   C. I'm going to start taking classes.

2. A. The class meets for 12 weeks.

   B. The class begins next Monday at 6:00 P.M.

   C. All computer classes cost $75.

3. A. I enjoy taking care of people and helping them.

   B. At night, I study English at Central Adult School.

   C. I want to go to college and study business.

Listening II [Tracks 18–20]

Listen. Questions 4 and 5 are on the audio CD.

Reading

Read. What is the correct answer: A, B, C, or D?

Greg has a job in an office. He organizes things, and he usually works alone. He doesn't like his job, but he isn't sure what he wants to do. He decided to take an interests survey to help him identify some of the things he's interested in and good at. The survey gave Greg some good information. He saw that he likes to work with other people. He's friendly and outgoing, and he's a good listener. He enjoys helping people and taking care of people.

---

6. What does Greg like to do?

    A. organize things

    B. work independently

    C. make friends and meet new people

    D. work with his hands

7. Which sentence is correct?

    A. Greg doesn't have a job now.

    B. Greg doesn't want to take an interests survey.

    C. Greg enjoys solving problems.

    D. Greg is good at listening to people.

Steve's Goals

	How will I achieve the goal?	When will I achieve the goal?
Short-term goal		
improve English to prepare for GED course	take intermediate ESL courses at Central Adult School	finish by May 2010
Mid-term goals		
get GED	take GED course at Central Adult School	finish by September 2010
get accepted to Baxter Community College	complete application	send application by October 2010
Long-term goal		
get associate degree at Baxter Community College	study part-time (two classes a semester)	get degree in May 2013

8. What is Steve's short-term goal?

   A. to get his associate degree

   B. to get his GED

   C. to improve his English

   D. to finish by May 2010

9. What will Steve do to reach his long-term goal?

   A. study part-time

   B. complete the application

   C. get a job

   D. finish by May 2013

10. When does Steve plan to get his degree?

    A. an associate degree

    B. in May 2013

    C. by September 2010

    D. two classes a semester

GED (Graduate Equivalency Diploma) PREPARATION

Course Code: 270369 GED

Description: This course helps students understand important concepts in the subject areas of social studies, science, mathematics, reading, and writing in preparation for the GED test. Classes are available in English and in Spanish.

Prerequisites: Open only to students who have not finished high school. Students must be age 18 or older.

Location: L.A. Employment Center, 536 W. Washington Blvd., Los Angeles

Section	Days	Time	Dates
627	TWTh	6:00 P.M.–8:00 P.M.	Feb 03–March 24

11. Which subjects are studied in the GED class?

   A. English and Spanish

   B. GED

   C. English

   D. social studies, science, mathematics, reading, and writing

12. How old do students need to be to take the GED class?

   A. Students must finish high school first.

   B. 18 years old or older

   C. under 18 years old

   D. Anyone can take the class.

13. Which days does GED section 627 meet?

   A. Tuesday, Wednesday, Thursday

   B. Monday, Tuesday, Wednesday

   C. Monday through Friday

   D. Saturday and Sunday

When do you want to begin studying at Northern Community College? (check one)

☐ spring semester   ☑ fall semester   ☐ summer session

year   **2010**

Do you want to study full-time or part-time?   **part-time**

Why do you want to enroll at Northern Community College? Check all that apply.

☐ Personal interest   ☐ Earn a two-year degree

☐ Improve skills to get a job / new job / promotion   ☑ Earn a certificate (non-degree)

☑ Improve skills for current job   ☐ Unknown / other

☐ Transfer to another college/university

I certify that all information given on this application is accurate.

Signature: **Arturo Ramirez**   Date: **March 10, 2009**

---

14. When does Arturo want to begin college?

    A. spring semester, 2010

    B. fall semester, 2010

    C. summer session, 2010

    D. March 10, 2009

15. Why does Arturo say he wants to go to college?

    A. to improve his skills for the job he has now

    B. unknown / other

    C. to earn a two-year degree

    D. He loves to study.

Unit 2 Communicating with Others

Learn

Note	Casual conversation is usually about topics that aren't very important. People talk about the weather, their weekends, movies, or their families. They don't usually talk about politics, religion, or personal matters in casual conversation.

A **Match the questions and answers.**

_d_ 1. It's so hot today, isn't it?

_____ 2. Did you hear the big news story?

_____ 3. Do you have plans for the weekend?

_____ 4. How's school?

_____ 5. When did you move here?

a. Three years ago. And you?

b. No, what happened?

c. Great. I really like my classes.

d. It sure is.

e. Yes, I'm going to the movies on Friday.

B *PAIRS.* **Check your answers.**

> **Example:**
> A: It's so hot today, isn't it?
> B: It sure is.

Listen

 Listen. Match the topics to the conversations.

_____ Conversation 1

_____ Conversation 2

_____ Conversation 3

_____ Conversation 4

_____ Conversation 5

a. weather

b. work

c. movies

d. native countries

e. family

Practice

A Read each conversation. Check the comments that you could use to continue the conversation. Sometimes more than one comment is OK.

1. **A:** So, what do you do?
   B: I work at Centerville Hospital.
   - ☐ That's interesting. How long have you worked there?
   - ☐ Wow! I guess you make a lot of money.
   - ☐ Really? What do you do there?

2. **A:** How have you been?
   B: All right, I guess. But I've been really tired and not feeling well lately.
   - ☐ Well, you're getting older.
   - ☐ A lot of people have been getting sick lately.
   - ☐ I'm sorry to hear that.

3. **A:** How do you know Olivia?
   B: We go to school together. We're in the same English class.
   - ☐ That's interesting. Where do you take your classes?
   - ☐ Oh, how long have you been studying English?
   - ☐ That's good. Olivia really needs to improve her English.

4. **A:** How's your family?
   B: They're fine. Thanks for asking. How about yours?
   - ☐ Everyone is OK, thanks.
   - ☐ Well, you know how it is. We're busy with all the kids' activities.
   - ☐ Terrible. My wife is making me very unhappy. I really want a divorce.

B *PAIRS.* **Check your answers. Explain the problem with each comment that's not OK.**

> **Example:**
> *A: In number 1, the first and third comments are OK.*
> *B: Right. The second comment is not OK. You shouldn't talk about money.*

Make It Yours

A On another piece of paper, write four questions or comments you could use to start a conversation.

B *PAIRS.* Take turns starting a conversation using one of your questions or comments. Then switch partners and start another conversation.

BONUS *GROUPS OF 3.* What topics are OK for casual conversation in your country? Are they the same as the ones in the United States? Report back to the class.

Lesson 2 Giving and Responding to Compliments

Learn

> **Note** In the United States, family, friends, and close co-workers often compliment each other's appearance, skills, personality, clothing, and other things. When someone gives you a compliment, it's polite to thank the person. Then it's common to add a comment.

 22 **Listen and read the conversations. Then practice with a partner.**

1. **A:** Your baby is so cute!
    B: Thanks. He looks like his father.

2. **A:** Nice sweater.
    B: Thanks. Gray's my favorite color.

3. **A:** That's a cool jacket.
    B: Thanks. It's new.

4. **A:** Your hair looks great.
    B: Thank you. I like yours, too.

Practice

A   **Match the compliments with the best responses.**

___b___ 1. You're such a good cook.

_____ 2. Those are great shoes.

_____ 3. Your English is really good.

_____ 4. I like your backpack.

_____ 5. You draw really well.

a. Thanks. It's new.

b. Thanks, but you're a good cook, too.

c. Thanks. I got them on sale this week.

d. Thank you. I've been taking an art class, and I really like it.

e. Thank you. I've been studying a lot.

B   *PAIRS.* **Check your answers.**

C   *PAIRS. ROLE PLAY.* **Imagine you are good friends. Take turns reading the compliments and the responses.**

> *Example:*
>
> A: *You're such a good cook.*
> B: *Thanks, but you're a good cook, too.*

Make It Yours

PAIRS. **Practice giving compliments and responding. Say something nice about your partner's appearance, something he/she is good at, something you like about his/her personality, or something he/she is wearing or has. Take turns.**

Making and Responding to Apologies

Learn

Note *When you apologize, it's common to give a reason or excuse. If it's appropriate, you can also explain how you will try to fix the situation.*

 23 **Listen and read the conversations. Then practice with a partner.**

1. **A:** Sorry I couldn't go to lunch with you yesterday. I was really busy.
   B: It's OK. We'll go another time.

2. **A:** I'm really sorry I broke your umbrella. I'll buy you a new one.
   B: Thanks, but you don't have to do that. It was old.

3. **A:** I apologize, but I'm going to be late this morning. There's a lot of traffic. I'll be there in about half an hour.
   B: OK. Thanks for telling me.

Practice

A **Read the situations. Write apologies to complete the conversations. Include a reason or an offer to fix the problem.**

1. Situation: You got home late last night, so you didn't call your friend.

   You: _____ I'm really sorry I didn't call you last night. I got home late. _____
   Your friend: Thanks for telling me. I wondered why you didn't call.

2. Situation: You borrowed a classmate's notebook, and you forgot to bring it to class.

   You: _____
   Your classmate: OK. That's fine.

3. Situation: You have an appointment this afternoon with your son's teacher. You can't give your co-worker a ride home from work.

   You: _____
   Your co-worker: No problem. I'll take the bus.

4. Situation: You used your friend's pen, and you lost it.

   You: _____
   Your friend: Thanks, but that's not necessary.

B *PAIRS.* **Compare your answers with a partner. Then practice reading the conversations out loud.**

BONUS *PAIRS.* **Talk about a time you apologized to someone or someone apologized to you. What was the situation? Was the apology accepted?**

Learn

Note It's polite to send a thank-you note when someone gives you a gift, invites you to their home for dinner, or does something nice for you. Sometimes thank-you notes are typed, but usually they're written by hand, often on a note card. Begin a thank-you note with Dear and the person's name. Finish the note with a closing, such as Sincerely, Kind regards, or Love, and sign your name.

Read the thank-you notes. Then answer the questions on page 31.

Dear Jill,

Thank you so much for the beautiful sweater. I love the color. It's a perfect present, and it's one of my favorite birthday gifts. Every time I wear it, I'll think of you.

Sincerely,
Kim

Dear Aunt Linda,

Thank you so much for letting me stay with you while I was in Chicago last week. It was much more fun staying with you instead of in a hotel. Thank you for all the wonderful meals you cooked for me. I enjoyed spending time with you and the rest of the family. I hope you come visit me in New York sometime!

Love, Beth

Dear Tom and Karen,

Thank you so much for inviting us to your party last week. We were very happy to be part of your celebration. We enjoyed meeting your friends. Your home looked beautiful, and the food was delicious. We hope we can get together with you again soon.

Kind regards,
Peggy and Jim

Dear Mrs. Pardo,

Thank you so much for the help you have given my daughter Monica in mathematics. She has always had difficulty in that subject, and your patience has made such a difference in her progress this year. She now understands mathematics, and she is enjoying it, too. I believe that will help her forever.

Sincerely,
Isabel Montes

1. Which letter thanks someone for a gift? _____
2. Which letter thanks a teacher? _____
3. Which letter is written by an overnight visitor?_____
4. Which letter thanks someone for an invitation to an event? _____

Practice

Read the thank-you notes again. Complete the sentences. Circle *a*, *b*, or *c*.

1. Kim says the sweater is _____.
   a. her favorite color   **b.** perfect   **c.** a good size

2. The sweater was _____.
   a. a birthday gift for Kim   **b.** a present from Kim   **c.** a gift for Jill

3. Beth liked _____.
   a. her aunt's cooking   **b.** staying in a hotel   **c.** going to New York

4. Peggy and Jim enjoyed _____ at the party.
   a. dancing   **b.** meeting people   **c.** spending time with family

5. Isabel Montes thanks Mrs. Pardo for her _____.
   a. invitation   **b.** gift   **c.** help

6. Isabel Montes thinks Mrs. Pardo is _____.
   a. difficult   **b.** patient   **c.** different

Make It Yours

Write a thank-you note to someone. You can use real or made-up information.

BONUS   *PAIRS.* **Do people write thank-you notes in your country? When do people usually write them (for gifts, for helping someone, etc.)? Is the custom different from the way it is in the United States? Talk about your experiences.**

Unit 2 Test

Before you take the test

(A)(B)(C)(D) Use the answer sheet for Unit 2 on page 223.

1. Print your name.
2. Print your teacher's name.
3. Write your student identification number, and bubble in the information below the boxes.
4. Write the test date and bubble in the information.
5. Write your class number and bubble in the information.

Listening I [Tracks 24–27]

Listen to the first part of the conversation. What should the person say next: A, B, or C?

1. A. I'm sorry about your sweater.

B. Thanks. It's new.

C. It's my sweater.

2. A. No problem. We'll go another time.

B. I went to the movies this weekend.

C. Have you seen that new movie?

3. A. Well, he's not a very good worker.

B. Really? How much money does he make?

C. Oh, that's interesting. Where is he working now?

Listen to the sentence. Which of the following means the same as the sentence you heard: A, B, or C?

4. A. How are you doing?

   B. How was your weekend?

   C. Do you have plans for the weekend?

5. A. I apologize. I can't go to your party.

   B. Sorry you didn't go to the party.

   C. I don't want to go to the party.

6. A. I need a good jacket.

   B. My jacket is nice.

   C. I like your jacket.

🔊 **Listening III** [Tracks 32–35]

Listen. Questions 7, 8, and 9 are on the audio CD.

Reading

Read. What is the correct answer: A, B, C, or D?

Dear Mrs. Garnett,

I am writing to apologize because I couldn't come to English class last week. My mother was sick, and I was home taking care of her. I plan to return to class next week. I will see you then.

Kind regards,
Sun Lee

---

10. Who is this note for?

    A. Sun

    B. Sun's mother

    C. Sun's teacher

    D. the students

11. Why is Sun sorry?

    A. She was sick.

    B. She didn't go to class.

    C. She was late for class.

    D. She can't return to class next week.

Dear Susan,

Thank you so much for the pretty shirt.
I love the color. It's a beautiful gift,
and it's one of my favorite birthday presents.
I'll think of you every time I wear it.

Sincerely,
Nancy

---

12. What is Nancy thanking Susan for?

    A. a birthday present

    B. the color

    C. every time

    D. a birthday party

13. What will Nancy do when she wears the shirt?

    A. think of Susan

    B. thank Susan

    C. write to Susan

    D. apologize to Susan

Lucinda and her husband, Juan, are from El Salvador. They came to the United States two years ago. They wanted to learn English and get good jobs here.

Lucinda got a job in an office, and Juan has a job at a hotel. They speak English at work. They make small talk with other people there. They talk about books and movies they enjoy, news stories, the weather, and their weekend plans.

Lucinda and Juan want to improve their English. On Monday and Wednesday evenings, they go to school and study English. Lucinda is in the high-beginning class, and Juan is in the low-intermediate class. They do their homework on Tuesday and Thursday evenings.

14. What does Juan do?

A. He wants to learn better English.

B. He's in the low-intermediate class.

C. He does his homework at work.

D. He works at a hotel.

15. Which topic *isn't* OK for Lucinda and Juan to talk about at work?

A. a story they heard on the news

B. the weather

C. how much money they make

D. a movie they saw last weekend

Unit 3 The American School System

Lesson 1   American School Structure

Learn

People in the United States usually use ordinal numbers to talk about grades in school, for example, 1st grade, 2nd grade, 3rd grade (first grade, second grade, third grade). But cardinal numbers are used when the word grade comes first, for example, grade 1, grade 2, grade 3 (grade one, grade two, grade three).

A 🔊 CD1 TRACK 36 **Look at the chart of the U.S. educational system. Listen to the descriptions of the schools and read the chart. Start at the bottom and follow the arrows.**

Vocational or Technical School		Junior or Community College		University or College	
3 years	OR	1-2 years	OR	4 years	Post-Secondary School
Students learn the skills needed to do a specific job. They receive a certificate (but not a degree) when they graduate.		Students learn specific skills or prepare for university. They receive an associate degree or certificate when they graduate.		Students get a general education. They receive a bachelor's degree when they graduate.	

⬆

High School
grades 9-12
ages 14-18
Students receive a diploma when they graduate.

⬆

Middle School
grades 6-8
ages 11-14

⬆

Elementary School
grades kindergarten (K)-5
ages 5-11

⬆

Preschool
ages 2-5

B   **Read the information about education in the United States.**

> In the United States all children are legally required to attend school. Education before kindergarten, or preschool, is not required, but many parents send their children to preschool. In most states, children must begin kindergarten at age five or six. Attendance is required until age sixteen or eighteen, again depending on the state.
>
> Universities, colleges, and junior and community colleges are all institutions of post-secondary education. Universities and colleges offer bachelor's, or four-year, degrees. Universities also offer degrees after the bachelor's degree, or post-graduate degrees (such as master's and doctoral degrees). A junior or community college usually offers associate, or two-year degrees, but some also offer four-year degrees. In the United States we often use the word *college* for any of these institutions.
>
> At the college level, the terms *freshman, sophomore, junior,* and *senior* are used instead of grade numbers. A freshman is in the first year of college, a sophomore is in the second year, a junior is in the third year, and a senior is in the fourth year. These terms are also used at the high school level, but grade numbers 9–12 are also used here. For example, a *senior* in high school can also be called a *twelfth-grader.*

C   **Look at the chart in Exercise A and the information in Exercise B again. Read the statements. Circle *T* for *True* or *F* for *False*.**

1. All children in the United States are required to go to school.   **(T)** **F**

2. Parents can choose whether or not to send their children to preschool.   **T** **F**

3. A student in fifth grade is probably about five years old.   **T** **F**

4. Students attend elementary school before middle school.   **T** **F**

5. Students can get a certificate from a vocational or technical school.   **T** **F**

6. Students have to go to a two-year college before they can attend a university.   **T** **F**

7. When students finish at a university, they receive an associate degree.   **T** **F**

8. A junior in college is in the third year of college.   **T** **F**

> **Note**
> **> > > > >**
> *Many post-secondary schools are known by abbreviations. For example, FIU = Florida International University, UA = University of Alabama, and CCD = Community College of Denver.*

D   **Match each school to its abbreviation.**

_d_ 1. AU   a. Community College of Allegheny County

____ 2. CCAC   b. University of California

____ 3. ACC   c. Austin Community College

____ 4. UC   d. American University

Practice

A   **Match each question with the correct response.**

_c_ 1. What grade is your daughter in?

____ 2. Is your son in high school?

____ 3. Where did you get your computer technician certificate?

____ 4. Does your son go to college?

____ 5. Where did you get your associate degree?

____ 6. Is your son starting school this year?

____ 7. Do you have a bachelor's degree?

a. At Lakeside Technical Institute.

b. Yes, from Forrest College.

c. She's in fourth grade.

d. Yes. He's a sophomore at UCC.

e. Yes. He's starting preschool.

f. At Houston Junior College.

g. Yes. He's a junior at Franklin High.

B   *PAIRS.* **Check your answers.**

> **Example:**
> *A: What grade is your daughter in?*
> *B: She's in fourth grade.*

Make It Yours

GROUPS OF 3. **How is the school system in the United States different from the one in your country? Make a list of similarities and differences and share it with the class.**

BONUS   *GROUPS OF 3.* **Talk about some of the schools in your district. Do you have children who go to these schools? If so, are they in elementary, middle, or high school? What grades are they in?**

Learn

Note > > > > >
- Schools in the United States typically use report cards to report students' learning progress to their parents. Most schools use a grading system of A through F combined with a plus (+) or minus (−) sign, or a numerical system of 1 through 100 percent.
- In most elementary and secondary schools in the United States, the school year is divided into two semesters. Each semester is divided into two quarters. Report cards are usually given at the end of each quarter.

A **37** Sofia Vega is talking to her mother about her report card. Listen to their conversation. Complete the report card. Write Sofia's grades in English, math, and music.

Green Hills Junior High School
22 Wilson Road, Dallas, TX 75201

Sofia Vega	Grade: 8	HR: Mrs. Benson	Year: 2011 2012

Subject	Instructor	First Quarter	Second Quarter	Third Quarter	Fourth Quarter	Comments
English	Blair					Needs improvement.
Social Studies	Smith	B				Does not complete all assignments. Please call me.
Mathematics	Wheeler					Very careful and accurate work.
Science	Lin	C				Conference requested. Please contact me.
French	Rice	B				Needs to spend more time on homework.
Computer Science	Renwick	A				Pleasure to have in class.
Music	Rosario					Participates well in class.

Explanation of Grades:

A	97 100%	B	87 89%	C	77 79%	D	67 69%	F	0 59%
A	94 96%	B	84 86%	C	74 76%	D	64 66%		
A	90 93%	B	80 83%	C	70 73%	D	60 63%		

B **Look at the report card on page 41 again. Match the teachers'**
comments in the report card from Exercise A with their explanations.

_e_ 1. Needs improvement.

____ 2. Does not complete all
assignments.

____ 3. Very careful and accurate work.

____ 4. Conference requested.

____ 5. Needs to spend more time on
homework.

____ 6. Pleasure to have in class.

____ 7. Participates well in class.

a. It's nice to have Sofia in class.

b. Sofia needs to be more serious about her
homework.

c. Sofia pays attention to her work, and she
doesn't make a lot of mistakes.

d. Sofia doesn't always do her homework.

e. Sofia needs to do better in that class.

f. Sofia is an active part of the class.

g. The teacher wants to talk to Sofia's parents.

C **Look at the report card again. Answer the questions.**

1. In which classes do the teachers say Sofia needs to make changes?

_____

2. Which teachers want to talk to Sofia's parents?

_____

3. In which classes does Sofia receive good comments?

_____

D *PAIRS.* **Sofia got the following grades in her second quarter: English**
B, Social Studies B+, Mathematics B+, Science C, French B, Computer
Science A, Music A+. Put her grades in the correct column in the report
card on page 41.

E *PAIRS.* **In which classes did Sofia do better in the second quarter than**
in the first? In which classes did she do worse? In which did she do the
same? Write your answers on a separate piece of paper.

Listen

 38 **Kevin and Rachel are talking about their report cards. Listen to the conversation. Write their grades.**

	Kevin	Rachel
1. history	_____	_____
2. science	_____	_____
3. Spanish	_____	_____

Practice

A **39** **Emily and Justin are talking about their report cards. Look at the report cards and listen to their conversation. Then practice with a partner.**

Name: Emily Butler
Grade: 10

Subject	Grade
Math	B
English	B+
Science	A–
American History	B+
Spanish	A
Computer Science	B

Name: Justin Meeks
Grade: 10

Subject	Grade
Math	C
English	\
Science	B
American History	\
Spanish	\
Computer Science	B

Justin: How did you do in <u>math</u>?
Emily: <u>I did OK</u>. I got <u>a B</u>. How about you?
Justin: I got a <u>C</u>. What did you get in <u>English</u>?
Emily: I got <u>a B+</u>. What about you?
Justin: I got <u>an A</u>.

Helpful Expressions
✓ I did pretty well.
✓ I did OK.
✓ I didn't do too/very well.

B *PAIRS. ROLE PLAY.* **Practice the conversation in Exercise A. Use the information in the report cards. Switch roles.**

Make It Yours

GROUPS OF 3. **Talk about your favorite subjects in school. Why are/were they your favorites? What are/were your least favorite subjects? Why?**

Unit 3 Test

Listening I [Tracks 40–42]

Listen to the sentence. Which of the following means the same as the sentence you heard: A, B, or C?

1. A. My son is seven years old.

   B. My son is in seventh grade.

   C. My son is in elementary school.

2. A. What was your grade in science?

   B. Did you study science?

   C. When do you have science?

Listen to the first part of the conversation. What should the person say next: A, B, or C?

3. A. I'm going to study at a senior high school.

    B. I'm going to study at a junior high school.

    C. I'm going to study at a community college.

4. A. He got a B.

    B. He's in eleventh grade.

    C. He got good grades.

5. A. I have a degree.

    B. from Stalton College

    C. in 2008

🔊 **Listening III** [Tracks 47–50]

Listen. Questions 6, 7, and 8 are on the audio CD.

Reading

Read. What is the correct answer: A, B, C, or D?

Bedford High School

Name: Olivia Santos
Grade: 11

	First Quarter	Second Quarter
American History	C	C
English	A–	A
Computer Science	C+	C–
Math	B	B+
Science	B–	B+
Spanish	A–	A
Art	B–	B–

---

9. What did Olivia get in English in the second quarter?

    A. A–

    B. B

    C. A

    D. B+

10. In which class was Olivia's grade worse in the second quarter than in the first quarter?

    A. American History

    B. Computer Science

    C. Science

    D. Spanish

George Washington High School
11 Tustin Blvd., Los Angeles, CA 92000

Paul Edwards
Grade: 10
Year: 2011-2012

HR: Mr. Brown

Subject	Credit	Instructor	First Quarter	Second Quarter	Third Quarter	Fourth Quarter	Comments
Computer Science	1.0	Perez	A–				Very capable student.
Mathematics	1.0	Ortman	C				Needs to spend more time on homework.
English	1.0	Whitney	C–				Conference requested.
French	1.0	Raynaud	B				Participates well in class.
History	1.0	Stevens	B–				Works well in class.
Science	1.0	Roffolo	A–				Very careful and accurate work.

11. In which class does the teacher say that Paul has to make a change?

    A. Computer Science

    B. Mathematics

    C. English

    D. French

12. Which teacher wants to speak with Paul's parents?

    A. Perez

    B. Ortman

    C. Whitney

    D. Roffolo

Matt is a senior at Mountain View High School in Denver, Colorado. Matt is a good student, and he usually gets A's and B's on his report card.

Matt is thinking about his plans after he finishes high school. He wants to get a job as an auto mechanic, so he's planning to study at Rex Technical School. At that school he'll learn the skills he needs to become an auto mechanic. When he finishes studying at the technical school, he'll get a certificate.

13. What grade is Matt in?

A. senior high school

B. fourth grade

C. twelfth grade

D. a senior in college

14. What will Matt do first?

A. get a job

B. study at Rex Technical School

C. get a certificate

D. finish high school

Unit 4 Talking on the Phone

Calling Directory Assistance

Learn

> **Note**
>
> Directory assistance can provide you with residential (home) and business phone numbers. Dial 411, and an operator or automated (computerized) system will answer. You'll be asked for the city (and sometimes state) you want to call and the name of the person or business. (The operator will ask, "What listing?") You might also need to know the street name. Most phone companies charge for each call you make to directory assistance. For an extra charge, or cost, your call can be automatically connected to the number so you don't have to dial it.

 51 **Listen and read the conversation.**

Operator:	What city and state?
Caller:	<u>Miami, Florida</u>.
Operator:	What listing?
Caller:	Could I have the phone number for <u>Ruby's Restaurant</u>?
Operator:	One moment, please.
Caller:	Thank you.
Operator:	There's more than one listing for that name. Do you know the street name?
Caller:	Yes, it's <u>157th Avenue</u>.
Operator:	Thank you.
Recording:	For a charge of thirty cents, your call to <u>305-555-6976</u> can be automatically connected by pressing 1 now.

Practice

PAIRS. **Practice the conversation in Learn. Then make new conversations with the information below. Switch roles.**

1. Houston, Texas / Maria's Tacos / Lincoln Avenue / 512-555-0036
2. Los Angeles, California / New Styles Salon / Cabazon Avenue / 323-555-9945
3. Newark, New Jersey / Page Through / Broad Street / 973-555-2041
4. Chicago, Illinois / Gables Dental Clinic / Clark Street / 773-555-4764

Make It Yours

A **Write your city, name, street, and phone number on a small piece of paper. (You can use real or made-up information.) Your teacher will collect all the papers, mix them up, and pass them out again.**

B *PAIRS.* **Practice the conversation in Learn again. This time, use the information on the paper you were given. Switch roles.**

Lesson 2 Taking and Leaving Messages

Learn

A   **Listen and read the phone conversation.**

A: Hello?

B: Hi, this is Victor Clark. Can I please talk to David?

A: I'm sorry, but he's not here. Do you want to leave a message?

B: Yes, please ask him to call me back. My number is 512-555-2839.

A: OK. I'll give him the message.

B   **Listen to the phone conversation again. Read the message. Answer the questions. Then practice the conversation with a partner.**

> David,
>
> Victor Clark called. Please call him:
>
> 512-555-2839.
>
> Tina

1. Who called? _____

2. Who took the message? _____

3. Who should call back? _____

4. Whose phone number is 512-555-2839? _____

Listen

 Listen to the conversations. Answer the questions. Circle a, b, or c.

1. Who does the caller want to talk to?

   a. Maria   **b.** John   **c.** Dominic

2. What should Mr. Hung do?

   a. call Allison   **b.** leave a message   **c.** call Jeff Thompson

3. What should Samantha do?

   a. call Amy   **b.** give the message to Amy   **c.** wait for Amy's call

4. What should Bill do?

   a. call Sam back   **b.** wait for Sam's call   **c.** leave a message

Learn

Note — *If you're not sure what someone has said, you can ask questions to clarify, or check, the information. You can ask:* Could you repeat that? Could I have your name / number again, please? Could you spell your (last) name? Did you say . . . . ? *You can also repeat what the person said, for example:* That's . . . ? You said . . . .

A **54** **Listen and read the phone conversation.**

A: Hello. This is Kelly.

B: Hi. This is Jim Matthews from Rockton Company. May I please speak to Jack Dubois?

A: I'm sorry. He's not in. Would you like to leave a message?

B: Yes, please. Could you ask him to call me?

A: Of course. Could I have your name again, please?

B: Sure. It's Jim Matthews.

A: Could you spell your last name, please?

B: It's M-A-T-T-H-E-W-S. And I'm calling because I want to schedule a meeting.

A: OK. And what's your number, Mr. Matthews?

B: It's 305-555-2393.

A: OK, 305-555-2393. And you want to schedule a meeting. I'll give Mr. Dubois the message.

B: Thank you.

A: You're welcome. Good-bye.

B **54** **Listen to the conversation again. Notice how Kelly asks questions and repeats things to be sure she got the correct information. How many examples of clarification can you find? Circle them. Compare your answers with a partner.**

C **54** **Cover the conversation. Listen again. Fill in the message. Use today's date and the actual time.**

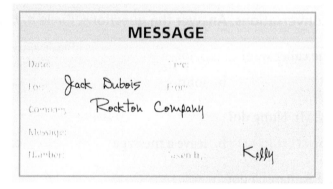

C *PAIRS.* **Check your answers. Then practice the conversation with a partner.**

Practice

 55 Listen to the conversations. Fill in the messages. Use today's date and the actual time.

1.

MESSAGE

Date: Time:
For: Mary Sanford   From:
Company: Bright Lighting Company
Message:
Number   Taken by: Tom

2.

MESSAGE

Date: Time:
For: Mr. Ting   From:
Company: Dr. Smith's office
Message
Number: Taken by: Nancy

Make It Yours

A   *PAIRS.* On a separate piece of paper, write a phone conversation. Use the conversation on page 52 as an example. Include clarification in your conversation. Practice reading your conversation out loud.

B   *GROUPS OF 4.* Join another pair of students. Pair A, read your conversation. Pair B, listen to the conversation and take a message. Use today's date and the actual time. Ask questions to confirm your understanding. Switch roles.

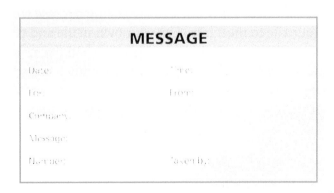

MESSAGE

Date: Time:
For: From:
Company:
Message:
Number: Taken by:

Learn

 56 **Listen to the message on Mr. Bower's answering machine. Check the information you hear in the boxes below. Check repeated information two times.**

Hello, this message is for Mr. Bower. This is Ramon Edulfo. It's 9:45 on Tuesday morning. I'm calling because there's a problem with my shower. My number is 301-555-4928. Again, my name is Ramon Edulfo, and my number is 301-555-4928. Thank you.

☐ ☐ who the message is for   ☐ ☐ the time of the call
☐ ☐ the caller's name   ☐ ☐ the reason for calling
☐ ☐ the caller's company   ☐ ☐ the caller's phone number
☐ ☐ the day of the call

Practice

57 **Listen to the message. Check the information you hear in the boxes below. Check repeated information two times.**

☐ ☐ who the message is for   ☐ ☐ the time of the call
☐ ☐ the caller's name   ☐ ☐ the reason for calling
☐ ☐ the caller's company   ☐ ☐ the caller's phone number
☐ ☐ the day of the call

Make It Yours

PAIRS. ROLE PLAY. **Student A, leave a message. Use the information below. You can use the message in Learn as an example. Student B, listen to the message Student A leaves. Write the information on a separate piece of paper. Switch roles. Check your answers.**

Student A: Leave a message for Daniel. You're calling because you're going to be half an hour late to meet him. Use your own name and phone number (or use made-up information). Use today's date and the actual time.

Student B: Leave a message for Dr. Taylor. You're calling because you want to schedule an appointment. Use your own name and phone number (or use made-up information). Use today's date and the actual time.

Learn

A   **Match the words and definitions.**

_d_ 1. option   a. times a store or business is open

____ 2. press   b. place

____ 3. location   c. dial by pushing a button on a phone

____ 4. hours   d. choice

B   **58**   **Listen. Which sentence do you hear? Circle *a* or *b*.**

1. **a.** To hear store hours, press 1.   **b.** For store hours, press 1.

2. **a.** To hear our location, press 3.   **b.** For our location, press 3.

3. **a.** To hear directions to the store, press 5.   **b.** For directions to the store, press 5.

Practice

 59   **Listen to the automated phone system message. Complete each sentence. Circle the correct word or phrase.**

1. The pharmacy is on **First Avenue and Rate Street / Second Avenue and Grand Street**.

2. If you are a **doctor / customer** press 9.

3. If you want to talk to **someone in the pharmacy / a doctor**, press 1.

4. If you have a question about **medicine / photos**, press 2.

5. If you want to talk to **a customer / someone in customer service**, press 3.

6. If you want to hear the pharmacy's **hours / location**, press 4.

7. If you want to **know when the store opens / talk to a manager**, press 5.

8. If you want to hear the options again, press the # / * key.

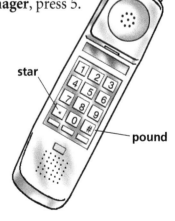

star

pound

Learn

A **Match the phrases and their meanings.**

_____ 1. repeat these options   a. talk to someone

_____ 2. for all other questions   b. if you have different questions

_____ 3. speak with a representative   c. hear the choices again

B **Read the message callers hear when they call the Tallville Electric Company. Complete the sentences.**

Thank you calling the Tallville Electric Company. Please listen carefully to the following options.

For service problems, press 1.
For billing and payment questions, press 2.
For all other questions, press 3.
To repeat these options, press 4.
To speak with a representative, press 0.

1. George has a problem with his service. He should press __1__.

2. Sun doesn't understand something on his bill. He should press ____.

3. Kim needs to talk to someone. She should press ____.

4. Mary doesn't remember what number to press for billing. She should press ____.

5. Ramon listened to all the options, but he has a different question. He should press ____.

Practice

60 **Listen to the automated phone system at Fleet City Power and Light Company. Answer the questions.**

1. If you have a problem with the service at your home, what should you press? ____

2. If you have a question about your bill, what should you press? ____

3. If you have to pay your bill late, what should you press? ____

4. If you are moving, what should you press? ____

5. If you want to listen to the options again, what should you press? ____

6. If you want to talk to a representative, what should you press? ____

Learn

Match the phrases and their meanings.

_d_ 1. for questions about billing

_____ 2. to request a catalog

_____ 3. to find a store near you

_____ 4. to place an order

_____ 5. for customer service

a. to hear the location of a store in your area

b. to ask for a book that shows the things a company sells

c. to get help from someone

d. to ask about a bill

e. to order something

Practice

A 🎵 **61** **Listen to the automated phone system message for Walcott's Department Store. Answer the questions.**

1. Mandy wants a catalog. Which option should she choose? _____

2. Tom wants to order something. Which option should he choose? _____

3. Elva wants to find a store. Which option should she choose? _____

4. There's a mistake on Franco's bill. Which option should he choose? _____

5. There's a problem with Delia's order. Which option should she choose? _____

B 🎵 **62** **Listen to the recorded message at the Douglas Museum of Science. Complete the information.**

1. location: _____ Fairview Avenue

2. hours: _____ to _____

3. ticket price for adults: _____

4. ticket price for children 3–17: _____

5. To find out about show times, press _____ .

6. To speak to a representative, press _____ .

7. To hear the information again, press _____ .

BONUS   **Do you prefer to use an automated system, or do you like to talk to a person? Why? Talk about your experiences.**

Unit 4 Test

Listening I [Tracks 63–66]

Listen to the sentence. Which of the following means the same as the sentence you heard: A, B, or C?

1. A. Mrs. Green isn't here.

   B. Mrs. Green is calling.

   C. Mrs. Green is on the phone.

2. A. Press 5 for the location.

   B. Press 5 to hear the options again.

   C. Press 5 to choose an option.

3. A. Press 1 to hear this number again.

   B. Press 1 to be connected to this number.

   C. Press 1, then dial this number.

You will hear a conversation or message. Then you will hear a question about it. What is the correct answer: A, B, or C?

4. Who should Hassan call?

    A. his boss

    B. Amir's wife

    C. Amir

5. What does Sue need to do?

    A. call Tom Nickels

    B. call Judy Smith

    C. take a message

🔊 **Listening III** [Tracks 70–73]

Listen. Questions 6, 7, and 8 are on the audio CD.

Reading

Read. What is the correct answer: A, B, C, or D?

MESSAGE

Date: _____ 8/6 _____   Time: _____ 9:15 _____

For: _____ Ms. Potter _____

From: _____ Diane Choi _____

Company: _____ D.A.C. Company _____

Message: _____ She needs William Lam's phone number. _____

_____ Please call her. _____

Number: _____ 410-555-2304 _____   Taken by: _____ Annie _____

---

9. Who called?

A. Ms. Potter

B. Diane Choi

C. William Lam

D. Annie

10. What should Ms. Potter do?

A. call Diane Choi

B. call William Lam

C. give Diane Choi the message

D. give Annie the message

Hi Lori,

Julie called you this morning.
She wants to have lunch with
you and Terri one day next week.
Sunday is a good day for Terri.
Are you available that day?
Please call back today.

Susan

11. Who should Lori call?

    A. Susan

    B. Terri

    C. Julie

    D. Julie and Susan

12. Why did the person call?

    A. She wants to have lunch together.

    B. She wanted to talk to Terri.

    C. She's not available on Sunday.

    D. She called this morning.

Thank you for calling the Ferris County Water Department. Please listen carefully to the following options. For billing assistance and questions, press 1. To report a problem with your water service, press 2. To speak to a representative, press 3. To repeat these options, press 4.

13. Becky needs to ask a question about last month's water bill. What number should she press?

    A. 1

    B. 2

    C. 3

    D. 4

14. Rick wants to talk to someone at the water department. What number should he press?

    A. 1

    B. 2

    C. 3

    D. 4

15. Angelica didn't hear the first option, so she wants to hear it again. What number should she press?

    A. 1

    B. 2

    C. 3

    D. 4

Unit 5 Community Information

Learn

A *PAIRS* **Read the first sentence in each item. Make the second sentence in each item have the same meaning as the first. Use the words in the box.**

past	light	Make	blocks	Head	onto	intersection	cross street

1. Go west. _____Head_____ west.

2. Turn right. _____ a right.

3. Turn left at the traffic light. Turn left at the _____.

4. Continue to go straight at the stop sign. Go _____ the stop sign.

5. Turn right, and you'll be on Grand Avenue. Turn right _____ Grand Avenue.

6. Go straight and cross two streets. Go straight for two _____.

7. Go to the place where Park and Oak meet. Go to the _____ of Park and Oak.

8. Spring Avenue crosses this street. Spring Avenue is a _____.

B 74 **Listen and check your answers.**

Practice

A **Look at the map on page 65. Read the directions. Answer the questions.**

1. You're at the Highton Hotel. Head north on Park. At the third cross street, turn right. It's the building on your left. Where are you? _____The Dental Office_____

2. You're at Cecilia's Café. Head west on Oak Street. Go past one traffic light. At the second traffic light, make a right onto Park Avenue. Go two blocks. Turn left onto Maple Street. It's on your right. Where are you? _____

3. You're at Gus's Gas Station. Head west on Maple to the end of the block, then south on Field for one block. Go west on Pine past two traffic lights. It's on your left after the second light. Where are you? _____

B *PAIRS.* **Check your answers.**

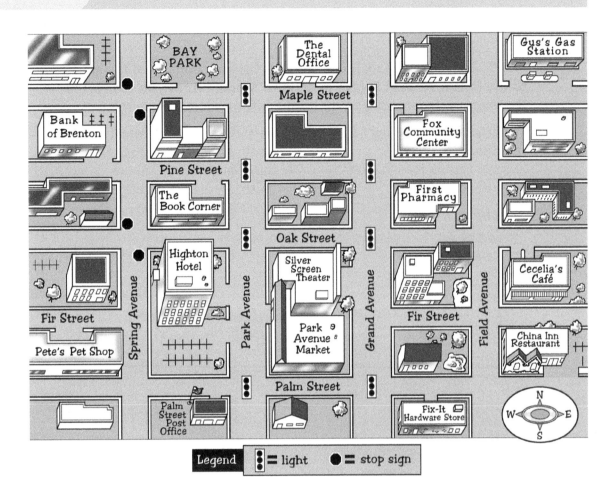

Legend   ⋮ = light   ● = stop sign

C   **Look at the map again. Complete the sentences. Use the words in the box.**

north	south	east	west	left	right

1. Mark is at the China Inn Restaurant. He wants to go to the Highton Hotel. He
   should head _____*west*_____ on Palm Street, then turn _____*right*_____ and go
   _____*north*_____ on Park Avenue.

2. Laila is at the Bank of Brenton. She wants to go to the Park Avenue Market. She should
   head _____ on Pine Street, then turn _____ at Park Avenue and go
   _____ .

3. Zoe is at the Silver Screen Theater. She wants to go to Fox's Community Center. She
   should head _____ on Grand, then turn _____ onto Maple.

4. Ahmed is at the Fix-It Hardware Store. He wants to go to the Book Corner. He should
   head _____ on Palm Street, and then make a _____ on Park Avenue.
   He should go _____ for two blocks on Park and then turn _____ .

5. Mateo is at Gus's Gas Station. He wants to go to the Highton Hotel. He should head
   _____ and go through one traffic light. At the second light he should make a
   _____ , and go _____ on Park.

D *PAIRS.* **Look at the map. Student A, ask for directions from the start to the finish. Student B, give directions. Student A, as you follow the directions, ask questions to clarify the information. Switch roles.**

1. start: Salem Elementary School
   finish: Salem Park
2. start: Farmer Joe's Market
   finish: Green Park
3. start: Bubbles Laundromat
   finish: Martin's Pharmacy
4. start: Salem Public Library
   finish: Fresh Coffee Café

Example:

A: Start at Salem Elementary School. Head south on Lily Street.
B: Did you say south?
A: Yes.

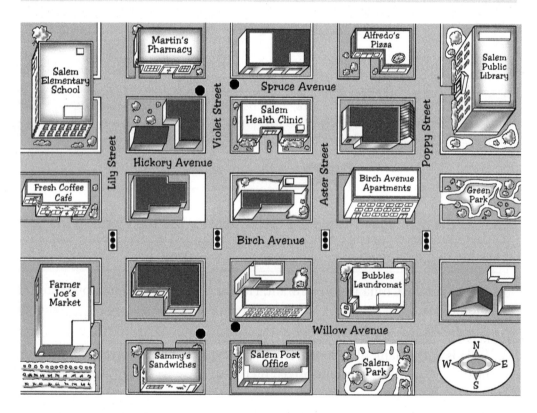

Make It Yours

A **Look at the map. Choose a place to start and a place to finish. Write down the directions.**

B *PAIRS.* **Student A, tell your partner where to start. Read your directions aloud. Student B, follow Student A's directions. If necessary, ask questions to clarify the information. When you finish, are you in the correct place? Switch roles.**

Listen

75 **Look at the map. Listen to the directions. Answer the questions. Circle *a*, *b*, or *c*.**

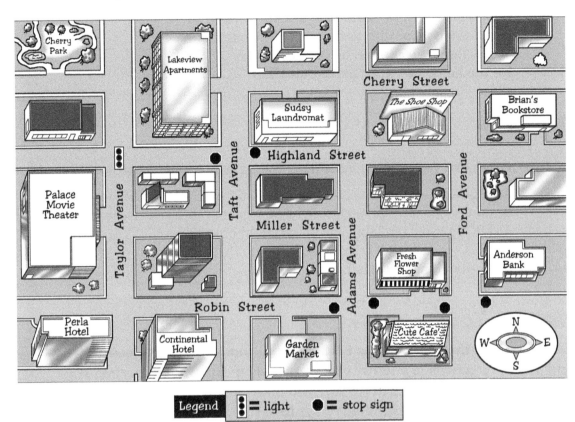

1. Start at Brian's bookstore. Listen and follow the directions. Where are you?

   a. Lakeview Apartments   **b.** The Shoe Shop   **c.** Anderson Bank

2. Start at the Palace Movie Theater. Listen and follow the directions. Where are you?

   a. Continental Hotel   **b.** Garden Market   **c.** Cute Café

3. Start at Anderson Bank. Listen and follow the directions. Where are you?

   a. Sudsy Laundromat   **b.** Garden Market   **c.** Lakeview Apartments

4. Start at the Perla Hotel. Listen and follow the directions. Where are you?

   a. Fresh Flower Shop   **b.** Brian's Bookstore   **c.** The Shoe Shop

5. Start at the Lakeview Apartments. Listen and follow the directions. Where are you?

   a. Cute Café   **b.** Perla Hotel   **c.** Fresh Flower Shop

6. Start at Garden Market. Listen and follow the directions. Where are you?

   a. Anderson Bank   **b.** Continental Hotel   **c.** Perla Hotel

7. Start at Cherry Park. Listen and follow the directions. Where are you?

   a. Palace Movie Theater   **b.** Sudsy Laundromat   **c.** The Shoe Shop

Learn

 76 **Listen and repeat ways to ask for directions.**

Can you tell me how to get to the Palace Movie Theater?
Could you give me directions to Brian's Bookstore?
What's the best way to get to the Perla Hotel?
Do you know how to get to the Cute Café?

Practice

 77 **Listen and read the conversation. Then practice with a partner.**

A: Excuse me. Can you tell me how to get to the Palace Movie Theater?
B: Sure. Go west on Robin Street. Make a right onto Taylor Avenue.
A: OK. I go west on Robin and make a right onto Taylor?
B: That's right. And it's the building on your left.
A: The building on the left. Great. Thanks.

Make It Yours

PAIRS. **Look at the map on page 67. Student A, choose a starting point and ask for directions to another place on the map. Follow your partner's directions. Ask questions to make sure you understand. Student B, give directions. Take turns. Use different ways to ask for directions.**

> **Example:**
>
> A: I'm at Brian's Bookstore. Could you give me directions to the Garden Market?
> B: Sure. Head west on Highland Street, then turn left and go south on Adams Avenue.
> A: Go which way on Adams . . . ?

Learn

A   **Read the library information.**

Sugar Valley   Public Library

Library Card Information

✗ Sugar Valley library cards are free to Sugar Valley County residents. To get a free library card, present one of the following: a driver's license, state identification card, recent utility or credit card bill, bank statement, rent receipt, or other document that shows your name and current address.

✗ Residents of other counties may get a library card for a fee of $20 a year.

Circulation Policy

The following rules apply to materials borrowed from the library:

✗ You may check out books, audio books, CDs, or videos for 3 weeks. DVDs and magazines may be checked out for 1 week.

✗ You may borrow a maximum of 20 books, 10 audio books, 10 CDs, 10 videos, 5 magazines, and 2 DVDs at one time.

✗ Books, audio books, CDs, and videos may be renewed for two weeks. DVDs and magazines may not be renewed.

✗ Library materials must be returned or renewed on or before the date they are due. The fine for overdue books, audio books, CDs, and videos is 10¢ per day. DVDs and magazines are $1.00 per day.

Computer Policy

Sugar Valley Library cardholders may use the library's computers to access the Internet as well as Microsoft Word and Excel programs free of charge. The following rules apply to the use of library computers:

✗ You must sign up before you use the computer. Reservations can be made online or in person at the library. You may reserve a computer up to one week before the date you want to use it.

✗ You may use the computer for one hour per day. At the end of one hour, if no one else is waiting, you may continue to use the computer for an extra hour.

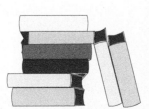

B Read the library information on page 69 again. Complete the sentences. Circle the correct words or phrases.

1. A resident of a place **works /(lives)**in that place.

2. When you check out materials, you **use them in the library / take them home**.

3. The maximum number of books is the **smallest / largest** number of books you can have.

4. When you renew library materials, you **return them immediately / keep them for a longer time**.

5. A fine is **money you pay when something is late / something you use at a library**.

6. The day your library materials are due, you have to **read / return or renew** them.

7. An overdue book is **late / free**.

8. When something is free of charge you **have to / don't have to** pay for it.

9. When you sign up for a computer, you put your name on a **list / library card**.

C Read the library information again. Complete the sentences. Circle *a*, *b*, or *c*.

1. You need to show _____ to get a library card.

   a. a photo   **b.** a driver's license and   **c.** a document with your
                                   a bank statement   name and address

2. A library card costs _____ if you don't live in Sugar Valley County.

   a. $20   **b.** $10   **c.** $0

3. You can borrow DVDs for _____.

   a. one week   **b.** two weeks   **c.** three weeks

4. You have to pay _____ per day for a late magazine.

   a. 10¢   **b.** $1.00   **c.** 50¢

5. Before you can use a library computer you have to _____.

   a. show your library card   **b.** access the Internet   **c.** make a reservation

6. You can use a computer _____ if no one is waiting.

   a. as long as you want   **b.** for an extra two hours   **c.** for an extra hour

Practice

A **78** **Listen and read the conversation. Then practice with a partner.**

A: Excuse me. I'd like to <u>renew these books</u>.
B: Sure. I can help you with that.
A: I have a question, too. How many <u>DVDs</u> can I check out?
B: You can borrow <u>two</u> at a time.
A: And how long can I keep them?
B: <u>Two weeks</u>.

B *PAIRS. ROLE PLAY.* **Student A, you need help at the library. Student B, you're the librarian. Practice the conversation in Exercise A again. Use the information in the boxes. Switch roles.**

1.
- sign up for a computer
- books
- 20
- three weeks

2.
- pay the fine for my overdue books
- magazines
- two
- one week

3.
- get a library card
- CDs
- five
- two weeks

4.
- check out these magazines
- audio books
- ten
- three weeks

Make It Yours

Look at the library information on page 69 again. Answer the questions.

1. You live in Sugar Valley. How much does a library card cost?

_____ It's free. _____

2. You checked out 3 CDs. How many more CDs can you check out?

_____

3. You have a DVD that is 2 days overdue. How much is the fine?

_____

4. You checked out a book on October 13. Today is October 25. Is the book overdue?

_____

5. You checked out a magazine on October 11. When is it due?

_____

6. You want to use a computer on October 31. What is the earliest day you can sign up?

_____

Learn

Read the information on the website. Then match the words and definitions.

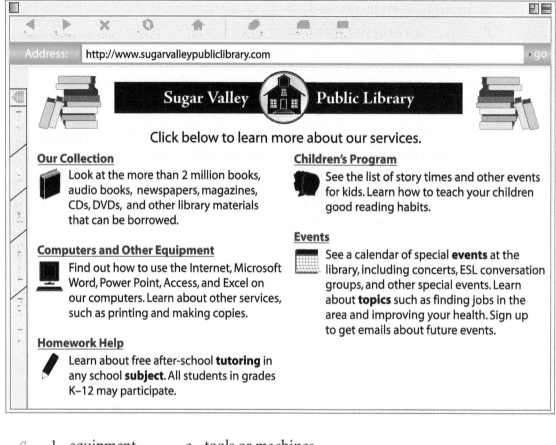

Address: http://www.sugarvalleypubliclibrary.com › go

Sugar Valley **Public Library**

Click below to learn more about our services.

Our Collection
Look at the more than 2 million books, audio books, newspapers, magazines, CDs, DVDs, and other library materials that can be borrowed.

Computers and Other Equipment
Find out how to use the Internet, Microsoft Word, Power Point, Access, and Excel on our computers. Learn about other services, such as printing and making copies.

Homework Help
Learn about free after-school **tutoring** in any school **subject**. All students in grades K–12 may participate.

Children's Program
See the list of story times and other events for kids. Learn how to teach your children good reading habits.

Events
See a calendar of special **events** at the library, including concerts, ESL conversation groups, and other special events. Learn about **topics** such as finding jobs in the area and improving your health. Sign up to get emails about future events.

_a_	1. equipment	a. tools or machines
___	2. tutoring	b. something people talk about
___	3. event	c. extra help with school work
___	4. topic	d. something special that is planned

Practice

Look at the website again. Read the sentences. Circle *T* for *True* or *F* for *False*.

1. You must bring your own computer to use the Internet at the library.   T (F)

2. Students can get help with their homework at the library.   T   F

3. You have to pay for tutoring.   T   F

4. Parents can learn how to help their children become better readers.   T   F

5. You can get information about jobs at the library.   T   F

Make It Yours

PAIRS. **Do you use any library services? Which ones? Which library services are you interested in learning about?**

Learn

A Look at some things you might need during or after an emergency. Which words do you know? Write the correct words under the pictures.

a wrench	batteries	non-perishable food	duct tape
a hand-crank radio	a first-aid kit	a can opener	hand wipes
a gallon of water	a dust mask	a whistle	a flashlight

1. _____

2. _____

3. _____

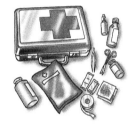

4. _____

5. _____

6. _____

7. _____

8. _____

9. _____

10. _____

11. _____

12. _____

B   **Read the article.**

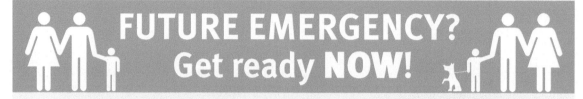

FUTURE EMERGENCY?
Get ready NOW!

> The best way you can help yourself and your family in an emergency is to plan *before* there is a problem. Every family should have an emergency kit, or set of things they can use in their home if there is an emergency. Here are some things you should have in your emergency kit.

WATER	Sometimes there isn't any water or the water isn't safe to drink after an emergency. For your kit you need one gallon of water per person per day. You should have enough water for three days (or more).
FOOD	You should have enough food for three days (or more). Put in your kit only non-perishable food that does not need to be refrigerated, such as canned or dried food. And don't forget a can opener!
FIRST-AID KIT	Make sure you have a first-aid kit. If someone gets hurt or sick in an emergency, you'll want to be able to take care of the person.
FLASHLIGHT AND BATTERIES	Sometimes the power goes out in an emergency. You should put a flashlight in your kit so you can see at night. It's a good idea to put extra batteries in your emergency kit, too.
HAND-CRANK OR BATTERY-POWERED RADIO	The radio is a good way to get instructions and information in an emergency. But many times there's no electricity, so make sure you have a hand-crank radio or one that uses batteries.
DUST MASKS	In some emergencies, the air might not be safe to breathe. You should have dust masks to wear if the air is bad. You should also have duct tape and large pieces of plastic to cover your doors and windows. That way it's harder for bad air to enter your house, and the air inside stays clean. 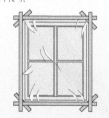
WRENCH	Some emergencies cause problems with the gas, water, or electricity in people's homes. You should have a wrench in your emergency kit to turn off the gas, water, or electricity in your house if necessary.
WHISTLE	After some emergencies, it might be difficult to leave your house. Put a loud whistle in your emergency kit. You can use the whistle to let others know that you need help.
HAND WIPES	Put hand wipes in your kit to clean your hands so you don't get sick.

Think about the needs of *all* your family members. Don't forget about things like prescription medication and, if you have a baby, diapers.

source: www.ready.gov

C   **Read the article again. Match the words and definitions.**

    c   1. gallon   a. a tool you use to turn something

        2. non-perishable food   b. a small battery-powered light you can hold in your hand

        3. first aid kit   c. a unit to measure liquids, equal to 4 quarts or about
                                        5 liters

        4. flashligh

        5. batteries   d. a thing that makes a noise when you blow air into it

        6. dust mask   e. food you can keep for a long time, not fresh

        7. wrench   f. something that covers your nose and mouth

        8. whistle   g. a set of things to take care of a person who is sick or hurt

                                       h. things that give electricity for lights, radios, etc.

Practice

Read the article again. Answer the questions. Circle *a*, *b*, or *c*.

1. When should you make an emergency kit?

    a. before an emergency   **b.** during an emergency   **c.** after an emergency

2. Which food is *not* good to put in an emergency kit?

    a. a can of beans   **b.** dried apples   **c.** a bottle of milk

3. Which two items in the emergency kit might need batteries?

    a. a can opener   **b.** a first aid kit   **c.** a flashlight
       and a flashlight   and a can opener   and a radio

4. Which of these things can help you communicate with people after an emergency?

    a. a whistle   **b.** a wrench   **c.** a first aid kit

5. Which things can help keep the air clean in your house?

    a. dusk masks   **b.** plastic and duct tape   **c.** hand wipes

Make It Yours

PAIRS. **Do you have an emergency kit? What's in it? Do you need to add anything from the article to your kit? What else do you think you need?**

> **BONUS**   **How much water do you need in your family's emergency kit? (Remember, you should have one gallon for each person per day for three days.)**

Unit 5 Test

Listening I [Tracks 79–82]

You will hear a conversation. Then you will hear a question about the conversation. What is the correct answer: A, B, or C?

1. Where does the man want to go?

    A. to the bank

    B. to the library

    C. to the park

2. What should the woman do first?

    A. go south on Main Street

    B. turn left onto Front Avenue

    C. go south on Front Avenue

3. What does the man need to do?

    A. renew some books

    B. return some books

    C. check out some books for class

Listening II [Tracks 83–86]

Listen. Questions 4, 5, and 6 are on the audio CD.

Reading

Read. What is the correct answer: A, B, C, or D?

Huntington Library

Rules for Materials Borrowed from this Library

- Books, audio books, CDs, and videos may be borrowed for three weeks.

- A maximum of 10 books, 5 audio books, 5 CDs, 5 videos, and 3 DVDs may be checked out at one time.

- All materials may be renewed for two weeks.

- Overdue fines are 10¢ per day for books and audio books. Fines for CDs, videos, and DVDs are $1.00 per day for each item.

---

7. How many books can you take from the library at one time?

    A. You can borrow books and audio books.

    B. You can renew books for two weeks.

    C. You can check out books for three weeks.

    D. You can check out 10 books.

8. How much do you have to pay if you return a CD late?

    A. $1.00 per day

    B. 10¢ per day

    C. three weeks

    D. a maximum of 5 CDs

✚ How to Make an Emergency Kit

Are you prepared?

Here are some things every family needs to have ready for an emergency:

1. **Water** Sometimes the water from your sink is bad after an emergency. Have enough water for three days. Each person needs 1 gallon of water per day.
2. **Food** Sometimes there's no electricity after an emergency. Without electricity, your refrigerator won't work. The food inside won't stay cold, and it could go bad. Have enough non-perishable canned or dried food for three days in your kit. Include a can opener if you have canned foods.
3. **Flashlight and batteries** If you don't have electricity, you can't turn on lights. Include a flashlight and the correct size batteries in your kit. Buy several extra sets of batteries.
4. **First-aid kit** Prepare a basic first-aid kit with medical supplies. Include pain relievers.

---

9. What is the purpose of this information?

   A. to explain what to do in an emergency

   B. to explain what to put in an emergency kit

   C. to explain how to make a first-aid kit for an emergency

   D. to explain how to use a first-aid kit in an emergency

10. How much water is needed per person for an emergency?

    A. 1 gallon each

    B. three days

    C. 1 gallon per person per day

    D. water for each person

11. What kind of food should be in an emergency kit?

    A. food in the refrigerator

    B. non-perishable food

    C. a can opener

    D. cold food

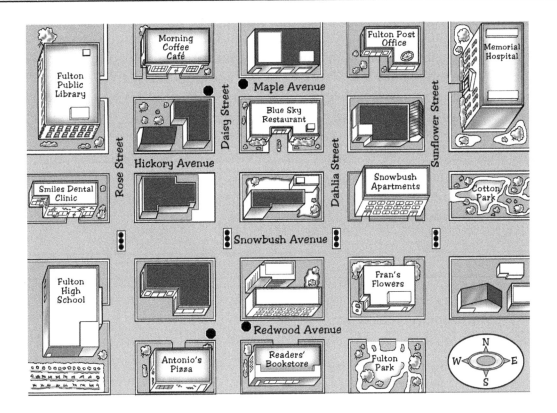

12. Where is the post office?

    A. It's at the intersection of Dahlia and Redwood.

    B. It's two blocks east of Morning Coffee Café.

    C. It's one block south of Snowbush Apartments.

    D. It's east of Memorial Hospital.

13. Start at the intersection of Redwood and Sunflower. Head west for two blocks and turn right at the stop sign. Go north for three blocks, and make a left on Maple. Which building is on your right?

    A. Fulton Public Library

    B. Fulton Post Office

    C. Morning Coffee Café

    D. Blue Sky Restaurant

14. How do you go from Smiles Dental Clinic to Cotton Park?

    A. Go north on Rose. Make a left on Walnut. It's on your right.

    B. Go east on Snowbush. Make a left on Sunflower. It's on your right.

    C. Go east on Snowbush. Cross Dahlia, and it's on your left.

    D. Go north on Rose. Then make a right on Maple. It's on your left.

Maria and Juan live in California. Sometimes there are earthquakes or other emergencies. If there is an emergency, Maria and Juan want to be ready. They have an emergency kit. They have water and non-perishable food in their kit. They also have a radio, two flashlights, and extra batteries for both of these things. They made a first-aid kit with medical supplies. Maria takes prescription medication, and they put that in the kit, too. Maria and Juan have dust masks in their emergency kit, and they also have plastic and tape to cover their windows and doors.

Maria and Juan hope they never need to use their emergency kit. But if there is an emergency, they'll be ready.

15. Why do Maria and Juan have an emergency kit?

A. There was an earthquake, but Maria and Juan weren't ready.

B. They want to be ready for an emergency.

C. Maria takes prescription medication.

D. They hope they don't have to use the emergency kit.

Unit 6 Transportation

Lesson 1 Transportation Schedules

Learn

A 🔊 CD1 TRACK 2 **Look at the morning train schedule. Listen to the conversation and circle the departure time of the train.**

A: Can you tell me what train I can take from Hillsdale to San Francisco? I need to be in San Francisco by 8:15.

B: You can take the 7:28. It'll get you to San Francisco at 8:00. It's an express train.

Hillsdale	7:02	7:16	7:28		8:02	8:39	8:59	9:29
San Mateo	7:08		7:32	7:49	8:07	8:43	9:05	9:33
Burlingame	7:11		7:35		8:11	8:16	9:08	9:36
Millbrae	7:17	7:24		7:52	8:17		9:13	9:41
Bayshore	7:33			8:08	8:33		9:27	
22nd Street	7:39				8:39	9:00	9:32	
San Francisco	7:48	7:42	8:00	8:17	8:48	9:08	9:41	10:02

= Express trains

B 🔊 CD1 TRACK 3 **Listen to the conversations. Write the departure times of the trains you hear.**

1. _____ 2. _____ 3. _____ 4. _____

C **Look at the train schedule again. Answer the questions.**

1. Ray needs to be in San Francisco by 8:30 A.M. He lives in Burlingame. What is the latest train he can take? _____ the 7:35 train _____

2. Paola has to be in Bayshore at 8:15 A.M. She lives in San Mateo. Should she take the 7:32, 7:49, or 8:08 train? _____

3. Shen lives in San Mateo. He has to be in Millbrae by 9:30 A.M. What is the latest train he can take? _____

4. Ying has a doctor's appointment in San Francisco at 10:00 A.M. She lives in Millbrae. Which train should she take, the 9:13 or 9:41 train? _____

5. Ricardo has an appointment at 9:00 A.M. near the 22nd Street station. He lives in Hillsdale. Which train should he take? _____

D *PAIRS.* **Check your answers.**

Practice

4 Ravi is calling an operator at New Jersey Transit to get information about commuter train schedules. Look at the schedule and listen to the conversation. Then practice with a partner.

Trenton	7:16	7:26	7:53	8:09	8:13	9:36	9:54
New Brunswick		7:53					10:21
Metuchen		8:01	8:24			10:05	11:29
Metropark		8:06	8:29			10:10	11:34
Linden		8:17		8:38			11:45
Newark	8:15	8:38	8:50	9:00			12:01
New York City	8:35	8:58	9:12	9:22	10:05	10:50	12:20

A: Hello. Can you tell me what train I can take from <u>Trenton</u> to <u>New York City</u>? I need to be in <u>New York</u> by <u>9:00</u> tomorrow <u>morning</u>.
B: One moment, please . . . OK. The <u>7:16</u> train will get you to <u>New York City</u> at <u>8:35</u>.
A: Is that an express train or a local?
B: It's <u>an express</u>.
A: Great. Thanks.
B: You're welcome.

Make It Yours

PAIRS. ROLE PLAY. **Student A, you are calling for train schedule information. Student B, you are the operator. Practice the conversation above with different stations and times. Use the schedule and the places and times in the chart below. Switch roles.**

From	To	Need to arrive by
Trenton	Newark	9:30 A.M.
Metropark	New York City	12:00 P.M.
Metuchen	New York City	10:00 A.M.
Newark	New York City	12:30 P.M.

BONUS *PAIRS.* **Bring in schedules for buses and trains in your area. How are they different from the schedules in Learn and Practice? How are they similar? Use one of the schedules to role-play asking for and giving schedule information.**

Learn

A   *PAIRS.* **Which words do you know? Match the words with their definitions.**

__j__   1.   on time
_____   2.   canceled
_____   3.   delayed
_____   4.   depart
_____   5.   arrive
_____   6.   board
_____   7.   passengers
_____   8.   gate
_____   9.   estimated
_____ 10.   local time
_____ 11.   flight time

a.   get to a place
b.   people traveling on a bus, train, or plane
c.   place where people get on a plane
d.   time in a specific place
e.   late
f.   close to an exact time or number
g.   length of time a flight takes
h.   when a scheduled event won't happen
i.   leave
j.   at the correct or scheduled time
k.   get on a bus, train, or plane

Note
>>>>>

Occasionally, buses, trains, and flights are delayed or even canceled because of bad weather, mechanical problems, or heavy traffic. It's a good idea to check if your bus, train, or plane is departing on time before you leave for the station or airport. You can call the airline, bus, or train company, or look online to see if there are any changes.

B   CD1 TRACK 5   **Look at the departure information on a screen at an airport. Listen and read.**

Hartsfield-Jackson Atlanta Airport

North Star Airlines Departures				
Destination	**Flight**	**Time**	**Gate**	**Remarks**
Chicago	239	9:00 A.M.	78	delayed (9:40)
Dallas	302	7:50 A.M.	65	boarding
Denver	811	7:25 A.M.	54	delayed (8:10)
Miami	422	8:15 A.M.	72	cancelled
San Antonio	102	8:20 A.M.	98	delayed (9:15)
San Francisco	262	8:00 A.M.	85	boarding

Practice

A  **6** **Listen and read the conversations between a passenger and gate attendant. Then practice with a partner.**

A: Is Flight <u>239</u> to <u>Chicago</u> on time?
B: <u>No, it's delayed. It will leave at 9:40.</u>

A: Is Flight <u>302</u> to <u>Dallas</u> on time?
B: <u>Yes, it is. It's boarding now.</u>

B *PAIRS. ROLE PLAY.* **Student A, you're a passenger. Student B, you're a gate attendant. Make conversations like the ones in Exercise A. Use the information on the departures screen on page 84. Switch roles.**

C **7** **Listen to the flight announcement. Then answer the questions.**

1. What is the flight number? _____

2. What is the estimated flight time? _____

3. What is the estimated arrival time in Los Angeles? _____

Listen

8 **Listen to the announcements in a bus terminal, an airport, and a train station. Which sentence is correct? Circle *a*, *b*, or *c*.**

1. **a.** The bus to Boston will leave at 8:45.
   b. The bus to Boston will leave at 8:15.
   c. The bus to Boston will leave at 9:15.

2. **a.** Flight 202 has been canceled.
   b. Flight 202 is delayed.
   c. Flight 202 is on time.

3. **a.** The 10:22 train is canceled.
   b. The 10:22 train is going to Rockville.
   c. The 10:22 train is now boarding.

4. **a.** Some bus service to Chicago is canceled.
   b. All bus service to Chicago is on time.
   c. There is no bus service to Chicago.

5. **a.** All trains departing from Baltimore will be delayed fifteen minutes.
   b. All trains going to Baltimore will be delayed fifteen minutes.
   c. All trains leaving from Baltimore are canceled because of mechanical problems.

Learn

A   **9** Look at the picture. Listen, read, and repeat.

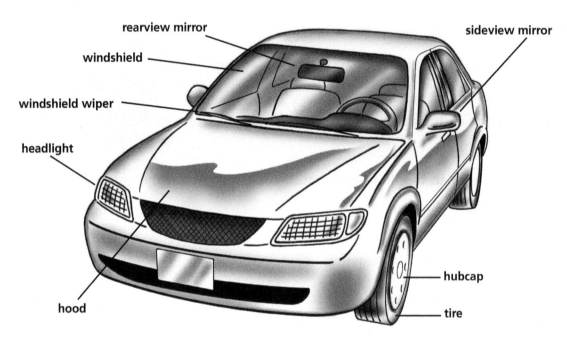

rearview mirror

sideview mirror

windshield

windshield wiper

headlight

hubcap

tire

hood

B   **10** Look at the picture. Listen, read, and repeat.

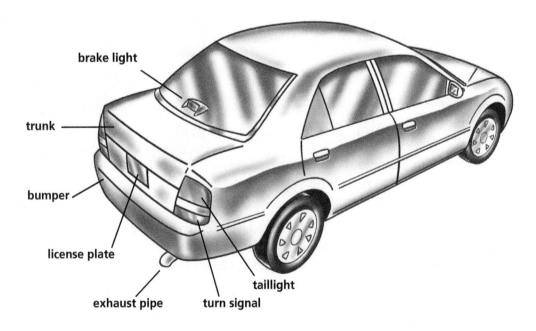

brake light

trunk

bumper

license plate

exhaust pipe

turn signal

taillight

Practice

A   Label the parts of the car. For an extra challenge, cover the picture in Exercise A on page 86.

headlight	hubcap	hood	rearview mirror
sideview mirror	tire	windshield	windshield wiper

B   Label the parts of the car. For an extra challenge, cover the picture in Exercise B on page 86.

brake light	bumper	exhaust pipe	license plate	taillight	turn signal	trunk

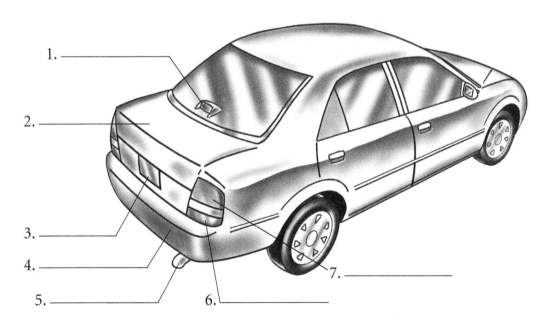

Learn

A   **Look at the picture. Listen, read, and repeat.**

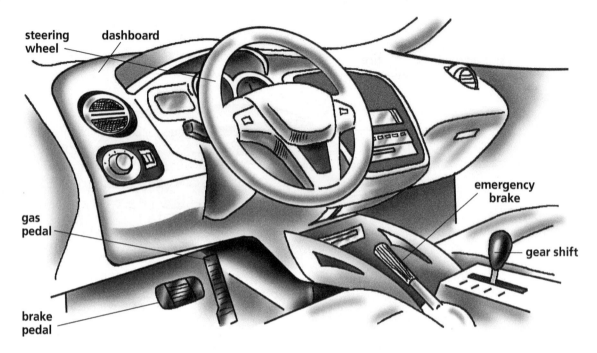

steering wheel

dashboard

emergency brake

gear shift

gas pedal

brake pedal

B   **Look at the picture. Listen, read, and repeat.**

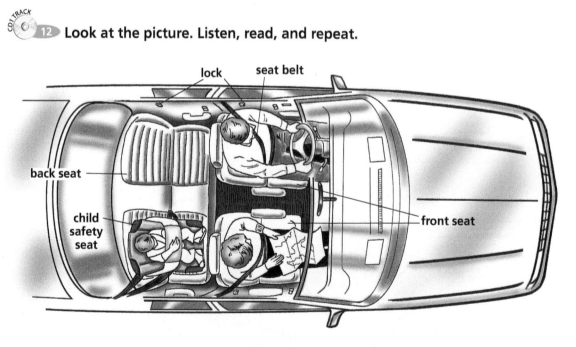

lock

seat belt

back seat

child safety seat

front seat

Note
>>>>>

In the United States, each state makes its own laws about seat belt requirements. In 49 states, seat belt use is mandatory. All 50 states require the use of a child safety seat, but laws based on the age and weight of the child vary from state to state.

Practice

A   Look at the picture in Exercise A on page 88 again. Match the words and their definitions.

_b_   1. dashboard

____ 2. steering wheel

____ 3. brake pedal

____ 4. emergency brake

____ 5. gas pedal

____ 6. gear shift

a. part of a car you press with your foot to make the car go faster

b. part of a car with controls and instruments to measure gas, speed, temperature, etc.

c. part of a car that the driver uses to change gears (gears allow you to go at different speeds)

d. separate brake system to use when the car is parked or when the regular brakes don't work

e. part of a car you press with your foot to stop the car

f. part of a car that you turn to control the direction of the car

B   Look at the picture in Exercise B on page 88 again. Match the words and their definitions.

_a_   1. seat belt

____ 2. front seat

____ 3. lock

____ 4. back seat

____ 5. child safety seat

a. part of a car that keeps a person safely in his/her seat in an accident

b. seat behind the driver

c. seat that keeps a baby or child safe in a car accident

d. the driver's seat and the seat next to it

e. thing that keeps a door closed

Make It Yours

GROUPS OF 3. **Talk about seat belts. Answer these questions:**

• Do you wear a seat belt? How often? If no, why not?

• Do you think seat belt laws for adults are a good idea, or do you think each person should be able to choose whether to wear a seat belt or not?

• What is your opinion of seat belt laws and safety seat laws for children? Explain.

Lesson 4 Car Maintenance

Learn

A Write the correct phrase under each picture.

check the tire pressure	get gas	add coolant and other fluids	check the oil

1. _____

_____

2. _____

_____

3. _____

_____

4. _____

_____

B   Listen and check your answers.

C Read the magazine article about car maintenance.

TIPS
for Taking Care of Your Car

Your car works best when it's in good condition. To avoid big problems and expensive car repairs, it's important to do some basic car maintenance regularly. Here are some of the things you should check:

- Check the tire pressure every week. (Your car's owner's manual will tell you what the tire pressure should be.) Look at the tires. Make sure they're not too old or worn. In addition, you should have your tires rotated, or their positions changed, every 7,000 miles.

- Check your car's oil every other time you get gas. Add oil if the level is low. Change the oil if it is black instead of a yellow brown color. In general, you should change the oil and oil filter every three months or every 3,000 miles.

- Replace your windshield wiper blades every six months. Don't wait until they break to change them. Check the level of windshield washer fluid every month. If the level is low, add more. Do *not* use water. Use washer fluid only.

- Check the levels of other fluids (liquids) such as coolant, or antifreeze, brake fluid, power steering fluid, and transmission fluid every other time you get gas. Add more fluid if the level is low. These fluids should be replaced about every 30,000 miles.

- Have a mechanic check your car's entire brake system every year.

D Read the magazine article again. Then match the words from the article with their definitions.

_h_ 1. repairs   a. change for something new

____ 2. maintenance   b. work that is necessary to keep something in good condition

____ 3. worn   c. liquid

____ 4. rotated   d. not in good condition because it has been used a lot

____ 5. level   e. moved or position changed

____ 6. replace   f. amount of something

____ 7. fluid   g. antifreeze, liquid that keeps a car engine cool

____ 8. coolant   h. things you do to fix something that's broken

E Read the article again. Read the sentences. Circle *T* for *True* or *F* for *False*.

1. You do maintenance to your car when it has a problem.   T (F)

2. Check the tire pressure every 7,000 miles.   T   F

3. Change your wiper blades before they're broken.   T   F

4. Change your oil and oil filter every other time you get gas.   T   F

5. Add oil to your car if the oil is black.   T   F

6. Add coolant to your car every week.   T   F

7. You can use water instead of windshield washer fluid.   T   F

8. The brake system should be checked every other year.   T   F

F *PAIRS.* **Check your answers with a partner. Correct the false statements.**

Example:

A: The first sentence is false.
B: Right. You do maintenance on your car before it has a problem.

Make It Yours

PAIRS. **Look at the maintenance tips on page 90 again. Do you do any of these things? How often? What other maintenance do you do on your car? Do you do the work yourself, or do you take your car to a service station?**

Lesson 5 · After a Car Accident

Learn

A   *PAIRS*   **Which words do you know? Match the words with their definitions.**

__g__   1. pull over

_____   2. injury

_____   3. ambulance

_____   4. exchange

_____   5. insurance

_____   6. record

_____   7. report

_____   8. tow truck

_____   9. within

a. vehicle that takes sick or injured people to the hospital

b. tell someone about something

c. an agreement with a company in which you pay it money regularly, and the company pays the costs if something bad happens to you or something you own

d. physical damage to a person's body caused by an accident

e. before a certain period of time ends

f. vehicle that takes a car to another place

g. move your car off the road

h. give something to someone who gives you something

i. write information about something

B   **Different states have different laws about what to do after a car accident. Read the information on one state's laws.**

What to Do after a Car Accident

- Stop. It's the law! You *must* stop if you are in an accident, even a small one. If you can, **pull over** to the side of the road.
- Find out if anyone is hurt. If anyone has serious **injuries**, call 911. Do not move a person with injuries. Wait for an **ambulance**.
- **Exchange** names, addresses, phone numbers, driver's license numbers, license plate numbers, and **insurance** information with the other driver or drivers. Also get the names, addresses, and phone numbers of other people who saw the accident.
- **Record** details of the accident as soon as possible. Write down everything you remember. If you have a camera, take pictures.
- Call your insurance company to **report** the accident.
- If you cannot drive your car away from the accident, you must call a **tow truck** to move it for you.
- If anyone is injured, report the accident to the police **within** 24 hours and to the Department of Motor Vehicles within 10 days.

If you have an accident with a parked car, leave a note with your name and telephone number on the windshield. It's against the law to drive away without leaving a note.

Practice

A **Read the accident information again. Complete the sentences. Circle the correct words or phrases.**

1. After an accident, you have to **drive away /(stop)**.

2. Call **your insurance company / 911** if anyone is injured.

3. It's a good idea to take pictures after an accident because it can help you remember **details of the accident / the other driver**.

4. Call **an ambulance / a tow truck** if you can't move your car.

5. Report an accident with injuries to **the police / the other driver**.

6. You can report an accident to the DMV **one week / one month** after the accident.

B **Read the accident information again. Read the sentences. Circle *T* for *True* or *F* for *False*.**

1. You don't need to stop after an accident if no one has injuries. T (F)

2. Call 911 even if the accident is small and there are no injuries. T F

3. You should move an injured person to a comfortable place. T F

4. You need to give your insurance information when you call 911. T F

5. You're not allowed to take pictures after an accident. T F

6. You can ask for a tow truck when you call 911. T F

7. You need to get the insurance information of all drivers in the accident. T F

8. If you have an accident with a parked car, you must leave a note on the car. T F

Make It Yours

GROUPS OF 3. **Have you ever been in a car accident? What happened? Who did you call? What did you do? Talk about your experiences. If you haven't been in an accident, talk about one you've seen or heard about.**

Unit 6 Test

> **Before you take the test**
>
> [A][B][C][D] Use the answer sheet for Unit 6 on page 231.
> 1. Print your name.
> 2. Print your teacher's name.
> 3. Write your student identification number, and bubble in the information below the boxes.
> 4. Write the test date and bubble in the information.
> 5. Write your class number and bubble in the information.

Listening 1

 Listening I [Tracks 14–17]

Listen to the sentence. Which of the following means the same as the sentence you heard: A, B, or C?

1. A. The train leaves Silver City at 7:42.

   B. The train arrives in Silver City at 7:42.

   C. The 7:42 train stops in Silver City.

2. A. Passengers have to go to Gate 202.

   B. Passengers on Flight 202 need to get on the plane now.

   C. Flight 202 is arriving at Gate 3.

3. A. The bus to Seattle is departing now.

   B. The bus to Seattle will leave late because of bad weather.

   C. No buses are going to Seattle because of the weather.

Listening II [Tracks 18–21]

Listen. Questions 4, 5, and 6 are on the audio CD.

Reading

Read. What is the correct answer: A, B, C, or D?

WE CARE

Auto Insurance Company

We hope you never have a car accident. But if you do, it's important to know what to do. If you're in any kind of an accident, follow these steps in order:

- Pull over immediately.
- Check for injuries. Call 911 if anyone is hurt.
- Get the names, addresses, and phone numbers of everyone who saw or was involved in the accident. Get insurance information, driver's license number, and license plate number from the other driver(s).
- Make notes about the accident. Write everything that happened. We'll need this information.
- Call WE CARE Auto Insurance Company to report the accident. We'll ask for your insurance information, as well as information about the accident.

7. What does this information explain?

    A. how to get information from other drivers

    B. how to report a car accident to the police

    C. what to do after a car accident

    D. why you should report an accident to your insurance company

8. What should a person do first after an accident?

    A. record details of the accident

    B. get out of the car

    C. talk to other people in the accident

    D. move the car off the road

9. Which part is the brake?

  A. Part A

  B. Part B

  C. Part D

  D. Part E

10. Which part is the steering wheel?

  A. Part A

  B. Part C

  C. Part E

  D. Part F

Greenboro	6:02 A.M.	6:16 A.M.*	6:28 A.M.*		7:02 A.M.	7:39 A.M.	7:59 A.M.	8:29 A.M.
Ridgeview	6:08			6:49	7:07		8:05	8:33
Mt. Rush	6:11		6:35		7:11	7:46	8:08	8:36
Fern Hill	6:17	6:24		6:52	7:17		8:13	8:41
Carmen	6:33			7:08	7:33		8:27	
King's Court	6:39				7:39	8:00	8:32	
Bayside	6:48	6:42	7:00	7:17	7:48	8:08	8:41	9:02

*Express trains

11. What time does the 7:02 train from Greenboro arrive at King's Court?

    A. 8:29

    B. 8:00

    C. 7:48

    D. 7:39

12. Which train is an express train?

    A. the 6:02 from Greenboro

    B. the 6:28 from Greenboro

    C. the 6:49 from Ridgeview

    D. the 8:29 from Greenboro

13. Dolores lives in Ridgeview. She needs to get to Bayside by 7:30. Which train should she take?

    A. the 6:16

    B. the 6:49

    C. the 7:07

    D. the 7:43

Kai-ying and Chen want to visit relatives who live in nearby cities on weekends. They decided to buy a car from their friend Marco, who is a mechanic. Marco explained some ways to help keep the car in good condition.

Kai-ying and Chen need to check the car's oil regularly. They should add oil when it's low and change the oil when it's black. They probably need to change the oil and oil filter about every three months. Kai-ying and Chen should also look at the levels of other fluids such as coolant, or antifreeze, brake fluid, power steering fluid, and transmission fluid about every two weeks. They need to put in more fluid if any of the levels are low. They should check the tire pressure when they get gas, or about once a week. It's important to have the brakes checked by a mechanic every year.

Marco told Kai-ying and Chen that if they take good care of the car, it will run well for many years. Kai-ying and Chen are very happy with their car, and they're going to take good care of it.

14. What should Kai-ying and Chen do when the car's oil level is low?

   A. change the oil

   B. check it when it's black

   C. add more oil

   D. check the oil regularly

15. How often should Kai-ying and Chen check the pressure of the tires?

   A. when they check the other fluids

   B. every two weeks

   C. when the fluids are low

   D. once a week

16. What maintenance do the brakes need?

   A. The brakes don't need maintenance.

   B. A mechanic should check them every year.

   C. Kai-ying and Chen should look at them every month.

   D. The car needs new brakes every year.

Unit 7   Money and Housing

Learn

A   **Match the words and pictures.**

a. ATM
b. cash
c. debit card
d. savings account
e. checking account

B   **Read the story.**

Sandra has two accounts at Fields Bank, a savings account and a checking account. She opened a savings account so that she could save some of her money and not spend it all. The bank pays her interest, or a small percentage of the money she keeps in that account. The interest rate is 4% a year. That means for every $100 she keeps in her account for a year, she will earn $4.

Sandra uses her checking account to pay for things. Sometimes she writes checks. Sometimes she uses her debit card. When she uses her debit card, the money is taken out of her checking account immediately. She can also use her debit card to withdraw, or take out, cash from her accounts at ATMs.

Sandra is happy about the services at Fields Bank. Her checking account is free. She has direct deposit, which means her employer can put her paycheck directly into her checking account. Fields Bank offers online banking, too, so Sandra can look at her account online and transfer money from one account into the other. She can use the ATMs at any Fields Bank free of charge, but she pays a $2 fee at other ATMs.

C   Read Sandra's story again. Match the words and definitions.

_e_ 1. savings account   a. move money from one account to another

____ 2. interest   b. an account that you can use to pay for things with checks
                                or a debit card
____ 3. checking account

____ 4. debit card   c. money that a bank pays you when you keep your money
                                there for a period of time
____ 5. withdraw
                             d. a way to take out money from an ATM and pay for things
____ 6. cash   directly from a checking account

____ 7. direct deposit   e. an account for money you want to save; it pays interest

____ 8. transfer   f. take out money from an account

____ 9. online banking   g. money you pay for a service

____ 10. fee   h. a way for your employer to put your paycheck directly
                                into your bank account

                             i. a way to get account information using the Internet

                             j. money (coins or bills)

Practice

**Look at Sandra's story again. Read the sentences. Circle *T* for *True*
or *F* for *False*.**

1. The bank pays Sandra money because she has money in her savings account. (T) F

2. Sandra can use her debit card to buy things.   T F

3. Sandra can use her debit card to get money from ATMs.   T F

4. Sandra pays $2 every time she uses an ATM at Fields Bank.   T F

Listen

CD1 TRACK 22 **Listen to the conversations. Match the topic to each conversation.**

____ 1. Conversation 1   a. savings account

____ 2. Conversation 2   b. free checking

____ 3. Conversation 3   c. withdraw cash

____ 4. Conversation 4   d. direct deposit

BONUS   Sandra earns 4% interest per year on her savings account. If she
keeps $200 in her savings account for a year, how much money
will she have in her account at the end of the year?

Learn

Note   *A + sign on a statement means money was put into the account. A – sign means money was taken out.*

A   **Sandra likes to do her banking online. Look at her online bank statement. Complete the sentences under the statement. Write the correct numbers.**

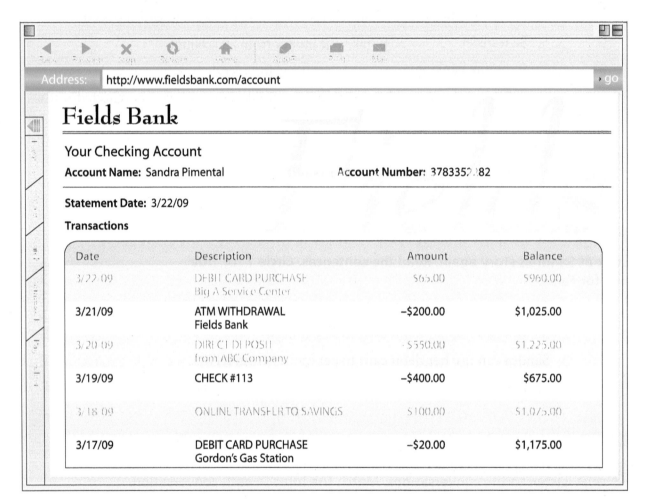

Address: http://www.fieldsbank.com/account   ▸ go

Fields Bank

Your Checking Account

Account Name: Sandra Pimental   **Account Number:** 3783352.82

Statement Date: 3/22/09

Transactions

Date	Description	Amount	Balance
3/22/09	DEBIT CARD PURCHASE Big A Service Center	$65.00	$960.00
3/21/09	ATM WITHDRAWAL Fields Bank	–$200.00	$1,025.00
3/20/09	DIRECT DEPOSIT from ABC Company	+$350.00	$1,225.00
3/19/09	CHECK #113	–$400.00	$675.00
3/18/09	ONLINE TRANSFER TO SAVINGS	$100.00	$1,075.00
3/17/09	DEBIT CARD PURCHASE Gordon's Gas Station	–$20.00	$1,175.00

1. How many times was money put into the account? _____

2. How many times was money withdrawn from the ATM? _____

3. How many checks did Sandra write? _____

B Look at the bank statement again. Complete the sentences. Use the words in the box.

balance	deposit	purchase	statement	transaction	withdrawal

1. Your _____*statement*_____ shows the money you have put into and taken out of an account during a certain period of time.

2. Any activity you do with your bank account is a _____.

3. When you make a _____, you buy something.

4. When you make a _____, you take money out of your account.

5. When you make a _____, you put money into your account.

6. Your _____ is the amount of money in your bank account.

Practice

Look at the bank statement again. Answer the questions. Circle *a*, *b*, or *c*.

1. How did Sandra make a payment to Big A Service Center?

   a. with a check 　　**b.** with her debit card 　　**c.** with cash

2. What was Sandra's account balance on 3/22/09?

   a. $65.00 　　　　**b.** $1,025.00 　　　　**c.** $960.00

3. How much money did Sandra take out from the ATM?

   a. $200.00 　　　　**b.** $1,025.00 　　　　**c.** $65.00

4. Who put money into this account?

   a. Sandra 　　　　**b.** ABC Company 　　　　**c.** Gordon's Gas Station

5. How much money was deposited into this account?

   a. $550.00 　　　　**b.** $1,025.00 　　　　**c.** $1,225.00

6. What was Sandra's balance after the deposit?

   a. $550.00 　　　　**b.** $1,025.00 　　　　**c.** $1,225.00

7. What was the amount of check 113?

   a. $675.00 　　　　**b.** $400.00 　　　　**c.** $100.00

8. On which day did Sandra move money out of this account into another one?

   a. 3/18/09 　　　　**b.** 3/20/09 　　　　**c.** 3/21/09

Make It Yours

GROUPS OF 3. **What are some advantages and disadvantages of online banking? Do you ever bank online? Why or why not?**

Learn

**Read the information about credit cards. Then complete the sentences.
Circle the correct words or phrases.**

> When you buy something with a credit card, you're borrowing money from the credit card company. Each month, the company sends you a bill for the things you bought with the card. You owe the company the amount on the bill. If you can't pay the full amount (all) of your bill, the company will let you pay only part of it, but each month you will have to pay interest (extra money) on the amount you still owe. The money you owe is the balance.
>
> You can also use a credit card to get cash from ATMs. This is called a cash advance. Credit card companies charge a fee for this service. You also have to pay interest on the money you take out until you pay back the full amount.
>
> Most credit cards have a limit on how much you can spend or withdraw. This is called your credit limit. You shouldn't spend more than that amount. If you do, you have to pay an extra fee.
>
> Credit cards are convenient, but they can be very expensive when you have to pay interest. So if you use a credit card, pay the whole bill each month. If you don't think you can do that, it's better to pay for things with a debit card. That way you can't spend more money than you have. For ATM withdrawals, it's also better to use a debit card, which takes money directly from your checking account and doesn't charge interest.

1. When you use a credit card to buy something, you borrow money from
   your bank account / the credit card company.

2. When you owe a person or a company money, you **have to pay / receive money from** the person or company.

3. Interest is money you **receive from / have to pay** a credit card company when you don't pay the full amount of your credit card bill.

4. The balance on your credit card is the amount you **already paid / still have to pay**.

5. Your credit limit is the **highest / lowest** amount of money you can spend with your credit card.

Practice

Read the story. Then read the sentences. Circle _T_ for _True_ or _F_ for _False_.

Two years ago, Kwan got a credit card to buy some things for his new apartment. The card had a $4,500 limit. After a few months, Kwan had bought too many things with his credit card. He couldn't pay the full amount of his monthly bill, so he only paid part. The credit card company charged him interest on the balance. Kwan continued to buy things with his credit card, but he didn't have enough money to pay the credit card bills.

One time, Kwan took money from an ATM with his credit card. He paid a cash advance fee and interest on the money. That was very expensive. Kwan's balance grew to $5,000. He went over the limit of his card, so he had to pay another fee.

Kwan realized he had a big problem: He owed the credit card company a lot of money. So he made some important changes. He stopped using his credit card. Every month he paid the credit card company as much as he could. After a year, Kwan had paid the balance on his credit card. Now he uses his debit card instead of his credit card because his debit card takes money directly from his checking account. That way, he can't spend more money than he has.

1. Kwan had to pay interest on the balance when he didn't pay the full amount of his bill.   (T) F

2. Kwan spent more money than he had.   T F

3. When he took money from an ATM with his credit card, Kwan paid a fee.   T F

4. Kwan had to pay a fee because his balance was more than $4,500.   T F

5. Now Kwan doesn't have a credit card problem.   T F

6. Now Kwan is using his credit card again.   T F

Make It Yours

GROUPS OF 3. **Talk about the advantages and disadvantages of credit cards and debit cards. Why do you think Kwan decided to use only a debit card? Talk about your own experiences using credit cards and/or debit cards.**

Learn

23 **Look at the credit card bill and explanations. Read and listen to the explanation of each part.**

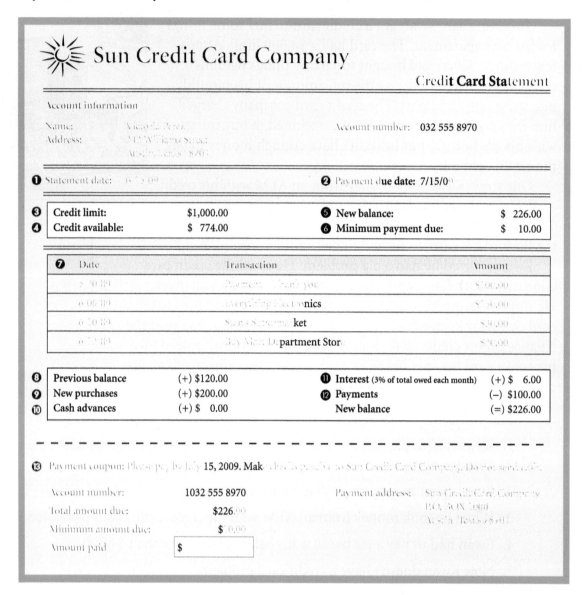

☀ Sun Credit Card Company

Credit **Card Stat**ement

Account information

Name: Victoria Perez   Account number: 032 555 8970
Address:

❶ Statement date: **❷** Payment due date: 7/15/09

❸ Credit limit:	$1,000.00	**❺** New balance:	$ 226.00
❹ Credit available:	$ 774.00	**❻** Minimum payment due:	$ 10.00

❼ Date	Transaction	Amount
	Payment – Thank you	
	Everything Electronics	
	Sun Supermarket	
	Buy Mart Department Store	

❽ Previous balance	(+) $120.00	**⓫** Interest (3% of total owed each month)	(+) $ 6.00
❾ New purchases	(+) $200.00	**⓬** Payments	(−) $100.00
❿ Cash advances	(+) $ 0.00	New balance	(=) $226.00

- -

⓭ Payment coupon: Please pay by July 15, 2009. Make checks payable to Sun Credit Card Company. Do not send cash.

Account number:	1032 555 8970	Payment address:	Sun Credit Card Company
Total amount due:	$226.00		P.O. BOX 1000
Minimum amount due:	$10.00		
Amount paid	$		

① day the credit card company sent you the statement

② last day you can pay this bill

③ total amount of money you can spend with this card

④ total amount you can spend with this card minus the amount you already owe

⑤ amount of money you owe the credit card company this month

⑥ smallest amount of money you can pay the credit card company

⑦ transactions made with the card this month

⑧ amount you owed last month

9 total amount you spent with the card this month

10 money you borrowed from your credit card company

11 extra money you have to pay because you didn't pay the full amount you owed last month

12 money you paid the credit card company last month

13 part of the bill you send to the credit card company with your payment

Practice

Look at the credit card statement again. Answer the questions. Circle _a_ or _b_.

1. What is the last day that Victoria can pay this bill?

    a. 6/15/09   **(b.)** 7/15/09

2. How much money in total did Victoria spend with her credit card this month?

    a. $150.00   **b.** $200.00

3. What is the total amount that Victoria owes the credit card company now?

    a. $226.00   **b.** $10.00

4. How much was Victoria's bill last month?

    a. $100.00   **b.** $120.00

5. How much did Victoria pay last month?

    a. $100.00   **b.** $120.00

6. Why does Victoria have to pay interest?

    a. because she didn't pay her whole bill last month   **b.** because she paid her bill late last month

7. How much does Victoria need to pay in interest this month?

    a. $6.00   **b.** $0.60

Note   *If Victoria doesn't make any new purchases with her card, and if she continues to make the minimum payment ($10) each month, it will take her about 31 months to pay the full balance on the card. By that time she will have paid $80 in interest in addition to the $220 for her purchases, for a total of $300!*

Learn

PAIRS. **Look at the ads for apartments for rent. Then look at the abbreviations. Which abbreviations do you know? Match the abbreviations to their meanings.**

FOR RENT

Redwood area. Lg. 2 BR, 1 BA

a/c, lg. yd., 1 car gar.

$975 incl. h/hw

623-555-1745 for appt.

FOR RENT

Downtown. $1,000 + util.,
2 BR, 1½ BA
new w/d, avail. immed.
great loc., nr. trans., 1 blk. to shops
1 mo. sec.
call 602-555-2938

__i__	1. lg.	a.	location
_____	2. BR	b.	including heat and hot water
_____	3. BA	c.	garage
_____	4. a/c	d.	near transportation
_____	5. yd.	e.	bedroom
_____	6. gar.	f.	available immediately
_____	7. incl. h/hw	g.	a security deposit equal to one month's rent is required
_____	8. appt.	h.	washer and dryer
_____	9. + util.	i.	large
_____	10. w/d	j.	yard
_____	11. avail. immed.	k.	the cost of utilities is extra
_____	12. loc.	l.	block
_____	13. nr. trans.	m.	air conditioning
_____	14. blk.	n.	bathroom
_____	15. 1 mo. sec.	o.	appointment

Note *Utilities are electricity, water, and gas. A half-bath has only a toilet and sink. A security deposit is money you pay when you move into a house or an apartment; you get it back when you move out if the house or apartment is in good condition and you have paid all your rent.*

Listen

24 **Listen to the conversations. What do you hear? Circle a, b, or c.**

1. **a.** two bedrooms   **b.** one bedroom   **c.** two bathrooms

2. **a.** $900 plus utilities   **b.** $900 including utilities   **c.** $900 security deposit

3. **a.** great location   **b.** two blocks from transportation   **c.** one block from a bus stop

4. **a.** near a park   **b.** garage   **c.** large yard

5. **a.** dishwasher   **b.** washer and dryer   **c.** heat and hot water

Practice

A   **Look at the apartment ads. Read the situation for each person or family. Match the people with the best apartment for them.**

a.

2 lg. BR 1½ BA

in nice area
a/c, w/d
$775 + util.
avail. immed.

b.

3 BR, 1 BA

$1,100 incl. h/hw

a/c, lg. yd., gar.

nr. schools, great loc.

c.

1 BR, 1 BA $675 + util.

2 blks. to park, nr. trans.

1½ mo. sec., avail. immed.

_____ 1. Marco and Lili have a nine-year-old daughter and a seven-year-old son. They want a place where the children can play outside. Marco and Lili can't pay more than $1,200 in rent. They're saving money because they plan to buy a car soon.

_____ 2. Jason is looking for a small apartment. He likes to exercise outside. He doesn't have a car. He can spend about $750 on rent and utilities.

_____ 3. Steve and Melissa are married, and Melissa's mother lives with them. They need an apartment next week. They can pay about $850 a month on rent and utilities.

B   *PAIRS.* **Check your answers. Explain your choice of apartment for each person or family.**

Make It Yours

PAIRS. **Bring in ads for apartments and houses for rent in your area. Find one you would like to live in. Tell your partner about the apartment or house.**

Lesson 4 Rental Agreements

Learn

> **Note**
>
> *A landlord is a person who owns an apartment or house that other people live in. A tenant is a person who rents an apartment or house. Both the landlord and the tenant must sign a lease before a tenant moves in. A lease is an agreement about the rules for renting an apartment or house. A lease is a legal document, often written in very formal language.*

A   *PAIRS.* **Look at the lease on page 111. Which words do you know? Match the words with their definitions.**

_e_	1. term	a. take care of something; keep it in good condition
____	2. premises	b. written information or warning that something will happen
____	3. due	c. permission
____	4. maintain	d. area around a building
____	5. alteration	e. period of time
____	6. consent (n.)	f. change
____	7. occupy	g. land or building that someone uses or lives in
____	8. notice (n.)	h. stay or live in a place
____	9. allow	i. do something that someone doesn't like
____	10. disturb	j. give someone permission to do something
____	11. grounds	k. needs to be paid

Lease Agreement

a. This agreement is signed on _____ between _____ _____ as landlord and _____ as tenant.

b. The term of this lease is for one year beginning on _____ and ending on _____.

c. The landlord agrees to lease to the tenant **the premises de**scribed as follows:

d. The tenant agrees to pay rent in t**he amount of** _____ per month, payment due on _____ **of each m**onth. All rent is to be paid directly to _____.

e. A late fee of _____ **will** be added for rent that is paid after _____ **of the mont**h.

f. The tenant **has paid a dep**osit of _____. At the end of the lease term, the la**ndlord will retu**rn to the tenant the total amount of the deposit if the premises **are in good cond**ition and the tenant does not owe unpaid rent.

g. **The tenant w**ill pay for all utilities provided to the premises.

h. **The ten**ant agrees to maintain the premises in good condition and will not make **any** alterations without the written consent of the landlord.

i. The tenant agrees that only those persons that have signed this lease will occupy the premises. Occasional overnight guests are allowed. Any one guest may not stay more than _____ nights within one month.

j. The landlord may not enter the premises without giving the tenant at least _____ notice, except in case of emergency. The landlord may enter to inspect, repair, or show the premises for sale or lease.

k. The tenant agrees not to make or allow any noise (shouting, singing, loud music or television, etc.) which would disturb other residents or neighbors.

l. The landlord agrees to maintain the building and grounds in a clean, safe condition.

B **PAIRS. Read part of a lease. Who is the tenant? Who is the landlord?**

Lease Agreement

a. This agreement is signed on _June 30, 2009_ between _Larry Olive_ as landlord and _Diane Popper_ as tenant.

b. The term of this lease is for one year beginning on _June 1, 2009_ and ending on _May 31, 2010_ .

c. The landlord agrees to lease to the tenant the premises described as follows: _269 Henry Street, Apartment 5C, Delray Beach, FL 33444_ .

d. The tenant agrees to pay rent in the amount of _$850.00_ per month, payment due on _the first day_ of each month. All rent is to be paid directly to _Larry Olive_ .

e. A late fee of _$30.00_ will be added for rent that is paid after _the fifth day_ of the month.

f. The tenant has paid a deposit of _$850.00_ . At the end of the lease term, the landlord will return to the tenant the total amount of the deposit if the premises are in good condition and the tenant does not owe unpaid rent.

g. The tenant will pay for all utilities provided to the premises.

h. The tenant agrees to maintain the premises in good condition and will not make any alterations without the written consent of the landlord.

i. The tenant agrees that only those persons that have signed this lease will occupy the premises. Occasional overnight guests are allowed. Any one guest may not stay more than _four_ nights within one month.

j. The landlord may not enter the premises without giving the tenant at least _24 hours_ notice, except in case of emergency. The landlord may enter to inspect, repair, or show the premises for sale or lease.

k. The tenant agrees not to make or allow any noise (shouting, singing, loud music or television, etc.) which would disturb other residents or neighbors.

l. The landlord agrees to maintain the building and grounds in a clean, safe condition.

Practice

A   Look at the lease on page 111 again. Read the sentences. Circle *T* for *True* or *F* for *False*.

1. Larry Olive is going to live in the apartment.	T	(F)
2. The lease is for one year.	T	F
3. The tenant has to pay $850 rent every month.	T	F
4. The tenant has to pay the landlord $30 if the rent is one day late.	T	F
5. The landlord will pay for heat and hot water.	T	F
6. The tenant has to ask the landlord before painting the apartment a different color.	T	F
7. Another person can move into the apartment with the tenant.	T	F
8. A guest can stay in the apartment for one week.	T	F
9. The landlord can't come into the apartment while the tenant lives there.	T	F
10. The tenant can't be loud.	T	F
11. The tenant has to keep the building safe.	T	F

B   Look at the lease on page 111 again. Answer the questions.

1. When does the lease start? _____

2. When does the lease end? _____

3. How much is the rent? _____

4. When is the rent due? _____

5. How much is the security deposit? _____

6. What two things must the tenant do to get the security deposit back at the end of the lease? _____ _____

7. Who has to pay for the electricity? _____

8. When is the landlord allowed to come into the apartment without permission?

_____

C   *PAIRS.* **Check your answers.**

Make It Yours

GROUPS OF 3. **Do you rent your apartment or house? Did you sign a lease? What are your responsibilities as a tenant? What are your landlord's responsibilities?**

BONUS   *GROUPS OF 3.* **Is your landlord a good landlord? Are you a good tenant? Talk about your experiences.**

Unit 7 Test

Before you take the test

A B C D Use the answer sheet for Unit 7 on page 233.

1. Print your name.
2. Print your teacher's name.
3. Write your student identification number, and bubble in the information below the boxes.
4. Write the test date and bubble in the information.
5. Write your class number and bubble in the information.

Listening I [Tracks 25–28]

You will hear a conversation. Then you will hear a question about the conversation. What is the correct answer: A, B, or C?

1. How does the man usually pay for things?

   A. with his credit card

   B. with his debit card

   C. with cash

2. What is the man going to do at the bank?

   A. put money into his account

   B. take money out of his account

   C. move money from one account to another

3. What does the woman have?

   A. a credit card

   B. a savings account

   C. a checking account

Listening II [Tracks 29–32]

Listen. Questions 4, 5, and 6 are on the audio CD.

Reading

Read. What is the correct answer: A, B, C, or D?

Back | Forward | Stop | Refresh | Home | AutoFill | Print | Mail

Address: @ http://www.neilsonbank.com ›go

Favorites | History | Search | Scrapbook | Page Holder

NB **Neilson Bank Online Statement**
Your Checking Account
Account Name: Victor Gomez   Account Number: 1346220875

Statement Date 06/14/09

Transactions

Date	Description	Amount	Balance
06/12/2009	ATM WITHDRAWAL First Bank	−$80.00	$405.00
06/11/2009	DEBIT CARD PURCHASE Stop-In Service Center	−$48.00	$485.00
06/10/2009	CHECK #92	−$200.00	$533.00
06/10/2009	ONLINE TRANSFER TO SAVINGS	−$130.00	$733.00
06/08/2009	DEBIT CARD PURCHASE Green Grocer Super Market	−$22.00	$863.00
06/08/2009	DIRECT DEPOSIT from Dalton Company	+$750.00	$885.00

---

7. On what date was money put into the account?

   A. 06/12/2009

   B. 06/11/2009

   C. 06/10/2009

   D. 06/08/2009

8. What was the balance after the ATM withdrawal on 06/12/09?

   A. $80.00

   B. $405.00

   C. $48.00

   D. $485.00

Two years ago, Ula was a student. She didn't make a lot of money, but she wanted to buy things, so she decided to get a credit card. Ula used her credit card to buy gas, food, and other things.

Each month, Ula got a bill from the credit card company, and each month she paid only the minimum payment. She was charged 12% interest each month on the amount that she didn't pay. She didn't think about the monthly interest charge on the credit card.

Ula's balance on the credit card grew quickly. She reached her credit limit in six months. With the interest that was added every month, she owed more and more. She saw that credit cards can be very expensive if you don't pay the balance every month. Ula decided not to use her credit card anymore. After she finished school and got a full-time job, she worked hard for the next year and finally paid off the balance.

9. What did Ula pay each month?

   A. the minimum payment

   B. the balance

   C. the interest

   D. the credit limit

10. Why did Ula decide not to use her credit card?

   A. She bought food with it.

   B. It was expensive.

   C. Her balance was low.

   D. She paid off the balance.

ORANGE CREDIT CARD COMPANY

CREDIT CARD STATEMENT

ACCOUNT INFORMATION:

Name:	Chen Tran	Account number: 1321 444 8067
Address:	151 Oak Street	
	Seattle, WA 98101	

Statement date:	09/12/10	Credit limit:	$500.00
Payment due date:	10/14/10	Credit available:	$225.00
		New balance:	$292.00
		Minimum payment due:	$ 15.00

Date	Transaction	Amount
9/02/10	Payment—Thank you	(−) $100.00
8/16/10	Great Buys	$100.00
8/10/10	Easy Gas	$25.00
8/02/10	Henry's Market	$25.00

Previous balance	(+) $220.00
New purchases	(+) $150.00
Cash advances	(+) $ 0.00
Interest (10% of total owed each month)	(+) $ 22.00
Payments	(−) $100.00
New balance:	(=) $292.00

11. What is the last day Chen can pay this bill?

   A. 10/14/10

   B. 09/02/10

   C. 08/10/10

   D. 09/12/10

12. What is the smallest amount that Chen has to pay this month?

   A. $100.00

   B. $15.00

   C. $500.00

   D. $292.00

Carol and Ray moved into a new apartment in San Diego. They were careful to read the rental agreement from their landlord before they signed it. The term of the lease is one year. It began on June 1. Carol and Ray agreed to pay $1,250 for rent each month, and they have to pay a late fee of $30 if they pay the rent more than five days late.

Carol and Ray agreed to some other rules, too, when they signed the lease. They have to keep the apartment in good condition, and they can't change anything in the apartment without the landlord's permission. Finally, they agreed not to make too much noise or bother their neighbors. Carol and Ray think that their new apartment is a great place to live.

13. What is the term of the lease?

A. a rental agreement

B. one month

C. one year

D. more than five days late

14. How much is the rent for the apartment?

A. June 1

B. $1,250 a month

C. $1,250 + $30 a month

D. $30 after five days

15. What do Carol and Ray need the landlord's permission to do?

A. make noise

B. keep the apartment in good condition

C. sign the lease

D. change anything in the apartment

Unit 8 Food and Shopping

Learn

 33 **Look at the measuring cups and spoons. Listen and repeat.**

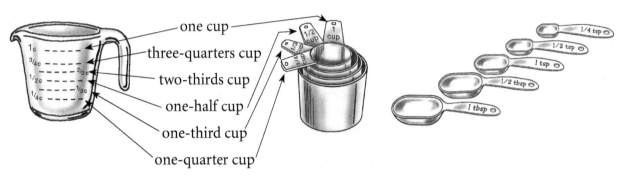

one cup
three-quarters cup
two-thirds cup
one-half cup
one-third cup
one-quarter cup

> **Note**
> >>>>> The abbreviation (or short form) for cup is c or C. Teaspoon is abbreviated tsp or t. Tablespoon is abbreviated tbsp or T.

Practice

Look at the amounts and the measuring cups and spoons below. Match.

_____ 1. 2 teaspoons

_____ 2. ¹/₂ cup

_____ 3. 1¹/₂ cups

_____ 4. 2 tablespoons

a.

b.

c.

d.

Make It Yours

Look at the measuring cups and spoons in Learn again. Answer the questions.

1. You need ²/₃ cup of sugar. Which dry measuring cup should you fill twice?

   _____

2. You need ³/₄ cup of flour. Which two dry measuring cups should you use?

   _____ and _____

Learn

Look at the pictures. Write the correct words from the box.

boil	chop	drain	melt	mix / stir	season	simmer	slice

1. _____simmer_____   2. _____   3. _____   4. _____

5. _____   6. _____   7. _____   8. _____

B   **Listen and check your answers.**

Practice

Match the words with their definitions.

_____ 1. drain	a.	change something from solid to liquid by heating
_____ 2. boil	b.	combine two or more ingredients, usually with a spoon
_____ 3. chop	c.	heat a liquid until it bubbles and starts to change into a gas
_____ 4. season	d.	cut food into thin flat pieces
_____ 5. mix/stir	e.	cook food slowly, by boiling it gently
_____ 6. melt	f.	add salt, pepper, etc., to food to make it taste better
_____ 7. simmer	g.	cut food into small pieces
_____ 8. slice	h.	make the water go out of something

Learn

A   Look at the food items in a recipe. Underline the amounts. Circle the ingredients.

1. 2 <u>pounds</u> (beef)

2. 2 teaspoons paprika

3. 3 tablespoons butter

4. 3 cloves of garlic, chopped

5. 2 cups beef broth

6. 1¹/₂ cups chopped green onions

7. 2 green peppers, cut into long pieces

8. ¹/₃ cup soy sauce

9. ¹/₃ cup water

10. 2 tablespoons cornstarch

11. 3 tomatoes, chopped

12. salt and pepper, to taste

B   *PAIRS.* **Check your answers.**

C Match the words and their definitions.

__d__ 1. paprika   a. a fine white powder used to make liquids in foods thicker

____ 2. cornstarch   b. a combination of two or more different things

____ 3. to taste   c. a flat heavy cooking pan with a long handle

____ 4. skillet   d. a red powder made from dried sweet peppers

____ 5. mixture   e. use an amount of something that tastes good to you

Practice

Read the recipe. Then answer the questions. Circle a, b, or c.

Pepper Steak

2 pounds beef

2 teaspoons paprika

3 tablespoons butter

3 cloves of garlic, chopped

2 cups beef broth

1½ cups chopped green onions

2 green peppers, cut into long pieces

⅓ cup soy sauce

⅓ cup water

2 tablespoons cornstarch

3 large, fresh tomatoes, chopped

salt and pepper, to taste

Slice steak into thin pieces, about a half-inch thick and 2 inches long. Season meat with paprika. In a large skillet, melt butter. Cook meat in butter until brown, about 5 minutes. Stir in garlic and beef broth. Cover and simmer 30 minutes. Stir in green onions and green peppers. Cover and cook 5 more minutes. Mix soy sauce, water, and cornstarch, and add mixture to skillet. Stir frequently as it thickens, about 5 minutes. Stir in tomatoes and heat through. Add salt and pepper to taste. Makes 4 servings.

1. What do you do before you melt the butter?

   a. Cut the meat.   **b.** Heat the paprika.   **c.** Stir the butter.

2. How long do you cook the meat, garlic, and beef broth?

   a. 5 minutes   **b.** 30 minutes   **c.** until it's heated through

3. What do you do first with the cornstarch?

   a. Add it to onions and green peppers.
   b. Mix it with the water and soy sauce.
   c. Stir it frequently.

4. When do you add the tomatoes?

   a. after the mixture thickens
   b. after the mixture is heated through
   c. after you add salt and pepper

Listen

35 Read the ingredients for making chicken fettucine alfredo. Then listen to the instructions. Number the pictures in the correct order.

> ## *Quick Home Cooking*
> ### *Chicken Fettuccine Alfredo*
>
> **You need:**
>
> 1 box of Quick Home Cooking
> Fettuccine Alfredo
> (includes pasta and seasoning)
>
> 1 lb. chicken, cut into 1 inch pieces
>
> 1 tbsp. oil
>
> 8 c. water
>
> ⅓ c. hot milk
>
> 3 tbsp. melted butter
>
> **Directions:**

a. _____

b. _____

c. _____

d. _____

e. _____

f. _____

BONUS

GROUPS OF 3. **Do you like to cook? Who usually cooks in your house? When you cook, do you usually follow a recipe? What is your favorite food to cook? Talk about your experiences with recipes and cooking.**

Learn

A   Look at the coupons. Then match the words and meanings.

_____ 1. manufacturer

_____ 2. expiration date

_____ 3. save

_____ 4. oz.

_____ 5. void

a. spend less money

b. cannot be used

c. abbreviation for *ounce*; a unit for measuring weight or liquid (There are 16 ounces in a pound.)

d. last day you can use something

e. company that makes a product

B   Look at the coupons again. Answer the questions.

1. What is another way to say *expires 12/31/10*?

_____ date 12/31/10

2. *MFR* is an abbreviation for _____.

Practice

Look at the coupons on page 125 again. Answer the following questions.

1. Can you use the coffee coupon to buy a 12-ounce can of coffee? _____

2. Can you use two coffee coupons to buy two cans of coffee? _____

3. Can you use the olive oil coupon if you buy one bottle? _____

4. Can you use two olive oil coupons? _____

5. Can you use a copy of the olive oil coupon? _____

6. How many bags of vegetables do you have to buy before you get a bag for free?
   _____

7. What size bag of vegetables do you get for free with the coupon? _____

8. What is the last day you can use the coupon for frozen vegetables?
   _____

9. Can you use the coupon for Sparkling Clean Glass Cleaner on a 16-ounce bottle?
   _____

10. Which coupon has the latest expiration date? _____

Make It Yours

PAIRS. **Look at the coupons on page 125 again. Read the information and questions below. Use the information to figure out the answers.**

1. A 39 oz. can of Drip and Brew Coffee costs $7.75. How much do you pay if you use the coupon? _____

2. A 16 oz. bottle of Regattori Olive Oil costs $4.50. How much do you pay for two bottles if you use the coupon? _____ A 32 oz. bottle of Regattori Olive Oil costs $8.35. Is it cheaper to buy two 16 oz. bottles with the coupon or the 32 oz. bottle without the coupon? _____ What is the difference in price?
   _____

3. A 16 oz. bag of Vita-Veg Frozen Vegetables costs $3.25. If you use the coupon, how much do three bags cost? _____

4. A 24 oz. bottle of Sparkling Clean Glass Cleaner costs $2.25. A 32 oz. bottle costs $2.75. With the coupon, which size bottle is cheaper? _____ How much does it cost? _____

BONUS **Do you use coupons? Which products do you use coupons for? Where do you get your coupons?**

Learn

Look at the ads. Then read the first sentence in each item. Make the second sentence in each item have the same meaning as the first. Use the words in the boxes.

SHOES ARE ON SALE!
Take **25%** off
every shoe in the store!

Men's Cruiser running shoes
Regularly $30. sale price this week:
just **$22.50!**

Women's Sweet Step shoes
Regularly $45. sale price this week:
just **$33.75!**

Great Discounts!
X Ladies' S.I.T. jeans
Regularly $25. now just **$20**!

X Men's Smart Look shirts
Regularly $20. now just **$15**!

X All kids' shirts and shorts are
on sale for just **$7** each!

Receive an additional $10 off any
purchase of $50 or more!

---

regularly	on sale	discount	sale price

1. During the sale, the price of shoes is 25% cheaper. There is a _____*discount*_____ on shoes.

2. Shoes are cheaper than usual. Shoes are _____.

3. The normal price of men's running shoes is $30. Men's running shoes are _____ $30.

4. There's a sale on Sweet Step shoes, and the price is $33.75. The _____ is $33.75.

---

just	off	purchase	additional

5. You can save $5 on men's shirts. Men's shirts are $5 _____.

6. Kids' shorts are only $7! Kids' shorts are _____ $7!

7. You can save $10 if you spend $50. You can save $10 if you make a _____ of $50.

8. Save an extra $10. Save an _____ $10.

Practice

A   **Read the department store ad. Then answer the questions.**

Big Deal Department Store
Back to School Sale!
Sat. 8/14 and Sun. 8/15

Shop before
12:00
and get an extra
$15 off
your purchase
of $35 or more!

40% off

all children's shoes.

Regularly $10.00–$30.00

Now just $6.00–$18.00

Show this ad
and receive
an additional
10% off
your entire
purchase!

25% off

all denim, including men's,
women's, and children's styles.

Regularly $13.00–$35.00

Now just $9.75–$26.25

30% off

all book bags, backpacks,
and lunch boxes.

Regularly $10.00–$30.00

Now just $6.30–$15.40

1. When is the sale? _____

2. What is the discount on children's shoes? _____

3. Are women's jeans on sale? _____

4. What is the sale price of the most expensive jeans? _____

5. What is the discount on backpacks? _____

6. What two things do you have to do to save $15? _____
   and _____

7. How can you get an extra 10% off you everything you buy? _____

B   *PAIRS.* **Check your answers.**

Follow these steps to figure out percent off an item.
1. Make the percent a decimal. For example, 30% = .30.
2. Multiply the price of the item by the decimal. For example, if an item costs $5.00, and it's 30% off, multiply 5.00 × .30. The answer is 1.50. So $1.50 is the amount off the regular price.
3. Subtract the amount off from the regular price to get the sale price of the item. For example, $5.00 − $1.50 = $3.50.

Make It Yours

PAIRS. **Look at the store ad in Practice again. Look at the regular prices of the following items. What is the price of each item during the sale?**

	Regular Price	Discount	Amount Off	Sale Price
1. boy's sneakers	$16.00	40%	$6.40	$9.60
2. girls' sandals	$13.00			
3. men's jeans	$33.00			
4. book bag	$19.00			

Listen

36 **Listen to each conversation. Which sentence is correct? Circle *a* or *b*.**

1. **a.** The shoes are 25% off.   **b.** The shoes are $25.
2. **a.** The shirt is 40% off.   **b.** The shirt is $40.
3. **a.** The jacket is $20 off.   **b.** The price of the jacket is $20.
4. **a.** You get an extra 10% off before 11:00.   **b.** The sale starts tomorrow at 10:00.
5. **a.** Women's pants are $10 off.   **b.** Women's pants cost $10.

BONUS

PAIRS. **Bring in ads from stores in your area. Ask each other questions about the ads. Take turns.**

Examples:

When does the sale start?
What is the discount on girls' dresses?
What's the sale price of children's sandals?
How much do men's T-shirts cost?

Learn

> **Note**
> >>>>>
> It's a good idea to do some comparison shopping before you buy things, and especially before you make big purchases. That can mean looking at the prices of the same item at different stores or online. You should also look at similar items and compare their features, or important details. Sometimes ads can help you comparison shop.

A **Look at two advertisements for vacuum cleaners. Which features are mentioned in the ads? Check the correct answers.**

❏ prices of the vacuum cleaners

❏ how long the vacuum cleaners will last

❏ other people's opinions of the vacuum cleaners

Dirt Vanisher

✳ low price—just **$145.99**

✳ lightweight and easy to carry up and down stairs

✳ great for removing pet hair from carpet and furniture

✳ dust and dirt stay in the bag so air is cleaner

✳ rated #1 vacuum by Customer Reviews magazine

Spiral Power Vac

$195.99

• quiet

• bagless—no dirty bags to change

• headlight helps you find every piece of dirt

• voted best vacuum by Educated Shopper magazine

B Look at the vacuum cleaner advertisements again. Answer the questions. Check *Dirt Vanisher, Spiral Power Vac,* or *Both.*

	Dirt Vanisher	Spiral Power Vac	Both
Which vacuum cleaner . . .			
1. is cheaper?	❑	❑	❑
2. isn't heavy?	❑	❑	❑
3. doesn't make a lot of noise?	❑	❑	❑
4. has a light?	❑	❑	❑
5. is a favorite of magazine readers?	❑	❑	❑

C *PAIRS.* **Check your answers.**

Practice

PAIRS. **Look at the vacuum cleaner advertisements again. Read the situations. Answer the questions.**

1. Yolanda has a dog and a cat. Which vacuum cleaner is probably better for her? Why?

   _____

2. Tom doesn't like to change his vacuum cleaner's dirty bags. Which vacuum cleaner is probably better for him? Why?

   _____

3. Dak-Ho and Sang-Mi live in a two-story house with carpet on the first floor and the second floor. Which vacuum cleaner is probably better for them? Why?

   _____

4. Sheila has a new baby. She likes to do housework while the baby sleeps. Which vacuum cleaner is probably better for her? Why?

   _____

Make It Yours

Look at the vacuum cleaner advertisements again. Imagine you're going to buy a new vacuum cleaner. Which vacuum cleaner is better for you? Why?

_____

BONUS *GROUPS OF 3.* **Do you comparison shop before you buy things? Talk about your experiences.**

Lesson 4 Making Returns

Learn

A *PAIRS.* **Which words do you know? Match the words with their definitions.**

___e___ 1. return

_____ 2. merchandise

_____ 3. refund

_____ 4. original

_____ 5. receipt

_____ 6. method of payment

_____ 7. store credit

_____ 8. exchange

a. take something back to a store and get something else in return

b. the first one; not a copy

c. a card or piece of paper worth a specific amount that you can use instead of money in a specific store

d. how you pay for something (cash, credit card, check)

e. take something back to a store

f. money that is given back to you when you return an item

g. a thing or things that are sold

h. a piece of paper that shows you paid for something

B **Match the words and pictures. Use the words in the box.**

exchange	refund	return	store credit

1. _____ 2. _____ 3. _____

4. _____

Practice

Read about returns at Book Central. Then answer the questions. Circle *a*, *b*, or *c*.

Book Central Returns

Customers may return merchandise within 60 days of purchase.

Refunds will be given for new merchandise with the original receipt. Refunds will be made in the original method of payment.

After 60 days, no refunds will be given. Merchandise may be returned for store credit or exchanged.

Customers returning an item without a receipt will receive store credit for the price of the item.

1. What information does the sign give?
   a. where to make a return
   b. the rules for making a return
   c. how to buy merchandise with store credit

2. What two things do you need to get a refund?
   a. new merchandise and the original method of payment
   b. new merchandise and the original receipt
   c. the original receipt and the original method of payment

3. What can you get if you return something after 60 days?
   a. a refund or store credit
   b. an exchange or a refund
   c. a store credit or an exchange

4. When will you receive store credit?
   a. when you return something with no receipt
   b. when you exchange something
   c. when you get a refund

Make It Yours

Look at the information about returns at Book Central again. Answer the questions.

1. You bought something at Book Central on April 15. Today is July 1. Can you get a refund if you return the item today? _____

2. You bought something with cash at Book Central on June 1. Today is July 1. Can you get cash back if you return the item today with your receipt? _____

3. You bought something at Book Central three months ago. Can you exchange the item for something else? _____

4. You want to return something to Book Central without a receipt. Can you get store credit? _____

Learn

A   **Read the information about warranties. Then read the sentences. Circle *T* for *True* or *F* for *False*.**

> A warranty is a company's written promise to fix or replace a product if it breaks within a certain period of time. (Warranties are often for one year, but they can be for longer, including "lifetime" warranties. A lifetime warranty usually lasts as long as the original owner, or the person who first bought the product, still owns it.) A warranty generally covers, or takes care of, problems caused by the company that made the product. Warranties usually do not cover any problems that are caused by using the product incorrectly.
>
> Many large stores offer customers the option to buy an extended warranty at an additional cost when they buy a product. When a customer buys an extended warranty, the store gives a warranty on the product for a period of time longer than the manufacturer's warranty.

1. A lifetime warranty lasts forever, even if the product is sold.   **T** (**F**)

2. Warranties usually cover problems that result from using a product incorrectly.   **T**   **F**

3. An extended warranty is usually included in the price of a product.   **T**   **F**

4. An extended warranty lasts for a longer period of time than a manufacturer's warranty.   **T**   **F**

B   **Complete the sentences with the words in the box. Use a dictionary if necessary.**

claim	commerical	damage	defect	defective	household	misuse

1. A _____*defect*_____ is a problem with a product caused by the company that made it.

2. A product that is for _____ use should only be used in a home, not a business.

3. When something is _____, it's broken or not working correctly.

4. When you make a warranty _____, you ask the company that made a product to fix or replace it.

5. A product that is for _____ use is good enough to be used in a business. In other words, it can be used more than a product for household use.

6. _____ is using something in an incorrect way.

7. When there is _____ to something, it is broken.

Practice

Read the warranty information. Then answer the questions. Circle *a*, *b*, or *c*.

1. What is explained in the warranty information?
   a. why the materials and workmanship of the product are good
   b. how to repair the product
   c. what the warranty covers

2. Where should this product be used?
   a. at Home Helpers
   b. at a business
   c. in a home

3. What will Home Helpers do if there is a problem with the product?
   a. give the customer a one-year warranty
   b. repair or replace it
   c. make the warranty void

4. What is required to make a warranty claim?
   a. materials and workmanship
   b. the original receipt
   c. a repaired product

WARRANTY:

Home Helpers products come with a one-year warranty against defects in materials and workmanship under regular, household use. Home Helpers will repair or replace the defective product covered by this warranty. Please keep your original sales receipt. You will need it to make a warranty claim.

This product is not for commercial use. Any misuse of the product will make this warranty void. The warranty does not cover damage caused by accidents.

Make It Yours

PAIRS. **Read the situations. Answer the questions.**

1. Your Home Helpers iron fell on the floor, and now it doesn't work. Does the warranty cover this problem? Why or why not? _____

   _____

2. After six months of normal use, one day your Home Helpers vacuum cleaner doesn't work. Does the warranty cover this problem? Why or why not? _____

   _____

3. You use the Home Helpers microwave in your business and it breaks. Does the warranty cover this problem? Why or why not? _____

   _____

BONUS *GROUPS OF 3.* **Have you ever made a warranty claim? Did the company fix or replace the product? Talk about your experiences.**

Unit 8 Test

 Listening I [Tracks 37–40]

You will hear a conversation. Then you will hear a question about the conversation. What is the correct answer: A, B, or C?

1. How much salt should the man add?

   A. a tablespoon

   B. a teaspoon

   C. half a teaspoon

2. What should the woman do first?

   A. add the tomatoes and simmer

   B. cook the onions

   C. chop an onion

3. How much can the woman save with the coupon?

   A. $30

   B. 30%

   C. $5

 Listening II [Tracks 41–44]

Listen. Questions 4, 5, and 6 are on the audio CD.

Reading

Read. What is the correct answer: A, B, C, or D?

Chocolate Chip Cookies

2 c. butter
2 c. sugar
2 c. brown sugar
4 eggs
2 t. vanilla
4 c. flour

1 c. oatmeal
1 t. salt
2 t. baking soda
2 t. baking powder
24 oz. chocolate chips

Mix butter, sugar, and brown sugar together. Add eggs and vanilla.
In a separate bowl, stir together flour, oatmeal, salt, baking soda,
and baking powder. Add flour mixture to butter mixture. Mix well,
about three minutes. Add chocolate chips. Place on cookie sheet
in small balls. Bake at 350 degrees for 12 minutes.

---

7. Which ingredients should be mixed first?

   A. flour, oatmeal, salt, baking soda, and baking powder

   B. all the ingredients together

   C. eggs and vanilla

   D. sugar, brown sugar, and butter

8. When should you add the chocolate chips?

   A. after adding the eggs and vanilla

   B. after stirring the flour, oatmeal, salt, baking soda, and baking powder

   C. after mixing all the other ingredients for three minutes

   D. after placing on a cookie sheet

KIDS' SUPER MART

Boys' sneakers 20% off
Regularly priced $20.00,
now just $16.00!

Girls' sandals 20% off
Regularly priced $16.00,
now just $12.80!

Backpacks 30% off
Regularly priced $15.00,
now just $10.50!

✂ –

Special Coupon!
One day only
Saturday, July 5

Save **$5.00** off your entire purchase with this coupon.

---

9. Which item has the most expensive sale price?

    A. the boys' sneakers

    B. the girls' sandals

    C. the backpacks

    D. the coupon

10. What is the sale price of the backpacks?

    A. $20.00

    B. $15.00

    C. $12.80

    D. $10.50

11. How much money can a customer save with the coupon?

    A. $20.00

    B. 50%

    C. $5.00

    D. 20%

Best Books

RETURN POLICY

Customers may return merchandise
within 30 days of purchase.
Refunds will be given only for merchandise
returned with the original receipt.
After 30 days merchandise may be returned
only for store credit or exchange.
Merchandise returned without a receipt may be
returned for store credit or exchange.

12. What can customers get when
they return an item with the
original receipt?

    A. a purchase

    B. a refund

    C. store credit

    D. an exchange

13. What can customers get when they
return an item without a receipt?

    A. exchange or store credit

    B. cash

    C. store credit only

    D. a refund

PRODUCT WARRANTY

Thank you for buying a Happy Home product. Our products come with a two-year warranty that covers defects in materials and workmanship under regular, household use. Happy Home will repair or replace the defective product covered by this warranty.

This product is for home use only. The warranty does not cover damage caused by accident or misuse of this product.

Please keep your original sales receipt from the purchase of this product. You will need it to make a warranty claim.

14. What does the warranty cover?

    A. defects in materials

    B. damage caused by accidents

    C. damage caused by misuse

    D. the original receipt

15. What will Happy Home do if a product is defective?

    A. give you a two-year warranty

    B. make a warranty claim

    C. replace or repair it

    D. give you a refund

Unit 9 Holidays, Government, and Law

Learn

> **Note**
>
> *In the United States, there are ten federal holidays set by law. Most of these (except New Year's Day and Christmas) honor, or show respect for, important people and events in American history. On federal holidays, government offices, most schools, and some businesses are closed, but stores are usually open. Other holidays, such as Valentine's Day, Mother's Day and Father's Day, and Halloween are celebrated by many people in the United States, but they are not official government holidays.*

Read about these U.S. holidays. Complete the information. Write the name of each holiday. Use the words in the box.

Christmas	Martin Luther King Day	Thanksgiving
Columbus Day	Memorial Day	Veterans Day
Independence Day	New Year's Day	Washington's Birthday
Labor Day		

1. January 1, or ___New Year's Day___, is a celebration of the start of a new year. Many people have parties in the evening on New Year's Eve, the day before this holiday. At midnight, everyone says "Happy New Year!"

2. On the third Monday in January, Americans celebrate _____. MLK Jr. helped to end segregation, or keeping white and black services, schools, and housing separate. He was killed in 1968. His "I have a dream" speech is the most famous American speech of our time.

3. On the third Monday in February, Americans celebrate _____. Many people call this holiday Presidents' Day. On this day we honor all U.S. presidents, especially George Washington and Abraham Lincoln. Washington was the first President of the United States (1789–1797). Lincoln was president during the Civil War (1861–1865). He is famous for ending slavery.

4. _____ is the last Monday in May. This is a day to honor Americans in the military who have died in war. Some people visit cemeteries and remember the people who gave their lives. This day is often considered the unoffical start of summer.

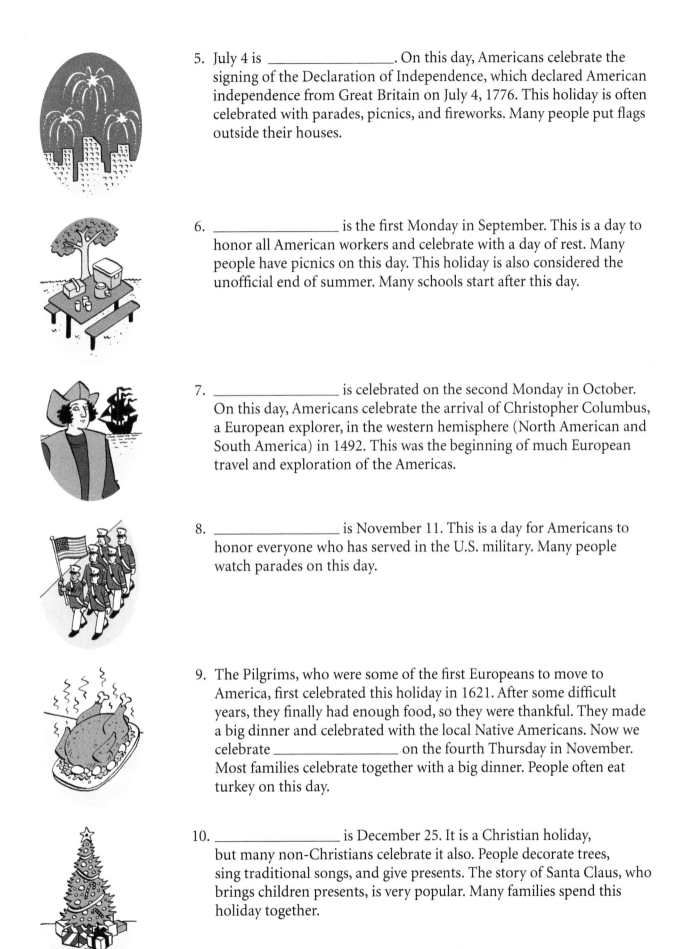

5. July 4 is _____. On this day, Americans celebrate the signing of the Declaration of Independence, which declared American independence from Great Britain on July 4, 1776. This holiday is often celebrated with parades, picnics, and fireworks. Many people put flags outside their houses.

6. _____ is the first Monday in September. This is a day to honor all American workers and celebrate with a day of rest. Many people have picnics on this day. This holiday is also considered the unofficial end of summer. Many schools start after this day.

7. _____ is celebrated on the second Monday in October. On this day, Americans celebrate the arrival of Christopher Columbus, a European explorer, in the western hemisphere (North American and South America) in 1492. This was the beginning of much European travel and exploration of the Americas.

8. _____ is November 11. This is a day for Americans to honor everyone who has served in the U.S. military. Many people watch parades on this day.

9. The Pilgrims, who were some of the first Europeans to move to America, first celebrated this holiday in 1621. After some difficult years, they finally had enough food, so they were thankful. They made a big dinner and celebrated with the local Native Americans. Now we celebrate _____ on the fourth Thursday in November. Most families celebrate together with a big dinner. People often eat turkey on this day.

10. _____ is December 25. It is a Christian holiday, but many non-Christians celebrate it also. People decorate trees, sing traditional songs, and give presents. The story of Santa Claus, who brings children presents, is very popular. Many families spend this holiday together.

Listen

45 Listen to the conversations. Match each picture to the correct conversation.

a.

b.

c.

1. _____   2. _____   3. _____

Practice

Look at the holidays on pages 142–143 again. Read the sentences below. Write the names of the holidays.

1. Americans often celebrate this holiday with fireworks and picnics.
   _____

2. On this start-of-summer holiday, some people visit military cemeteries.
   _____

3. Many American schools use this holiday to teach students the history of the presidents of the United States. _____

4. People give presents on this holiday. _____

5. This end-of-summer holiday is often enjoyed by relaxing and having picnics.
   _____

6. People prepare a large meal for their families on this holiday. They think about all the good things in their lives. _____

7. On this day, many people do work in their communities to honor the life of a great American. _____

8. People often have parties and start to celebrate this holiday the night before.
   _____

9. On this holiday, there are parades to honor Americans, living and dead, who have served in the military. _____

10. People think about one of the first Europeans who came to America on this holiday.
    _____

BONUS

GROUPS OF 3. **What other U.S. holidays do you know? What holidays do people celebrate in your country? When is each holiday? What or whom does the holiday celebrate or honor? What do people usually do on that day?**

Learn

A   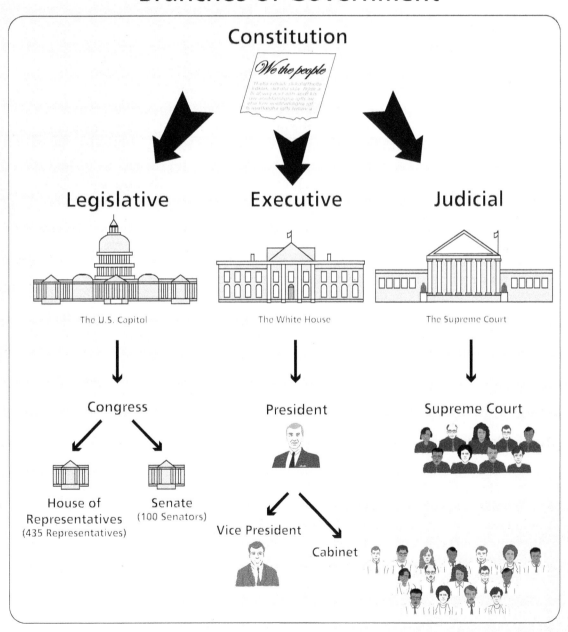 **CD 1 TRACK 46** **Listen and look at the diagram of the three branches, or parts, of the U.S. federal government. Listen and read.**

Note   *The federal government is the national, or central, government of the United States.*

Branches of Government

Constitution

We the people

Legislative   Executive   Judicial

The U.S. Capitol   The White House   The Supreme Court

Congress   President   Supreme Court

House of Representatives
(435 Representatives)   Senate
(100 Senators)

Vice President   Cabinet

B **Read the article about the U.S. Constitution and the three branches of government.**

The Constitution

The U.S. Constitution is the highest law of our country. Written in 1789, it explains:
- the three branches, or parts, of the federal government: the legislative branch, the executive branch, and the judicial branch.
- the system called "checks and balances," which makes sure no branch has too much power or control.
- the responsibilities of the federal government and state governments.
- the basic rights of Americans, or things that Americans are free to do. These rights are explained in a part of the Constitution called the Bill of Rights.

The Legislative Branch

The legislative branch is made up of the two houses of Congress: the Senate and the House of Representatives. There are 100 senators and 435 representatives. Congress writes bills and then votes on them. After Congress passes a bill, it goes to the president (who is part of the executive branch). If the president signs the bill, it becomes a law. If the president vetoes the bill, or doesn't sign it, it doesn't become a law. To override, or cancel, the president's veto, two-thirds ($^2/_3$) of all Congress members (66 senators and 286 representatives) must vote for the bill. In this way the president can "check" the power of Congress with a veto, but Congress can "check" the power of the president by overriding the veto. This system keeps a balance of power between the president and Congress.

The Executive Branch

The president is the head of the executive branch. He or she signs bills into laws or vetoes them. In addition, the president directs foreign policy (relations with other countries) and is commander in chief (leader) of the U.S. military. The president chooses cabinet members to direct different departments of the government. The vice president is part of the executive branch, and is also the leader of the Senate. The vice president becomes the president if the president dies. The president needs money to run the government. Only Congress can provide it. Here, Congress "checks" the executive branch through the power to control how money is spent.

The Judicial Branch

The judicial branch is made up of the Supreme Court and the lower federal courts. The Supreme Court is the most powerful court in the country. The president nominates (suggests) judges and the Senate approves them. The nine justices, or judges, on the Supreme Court decide if laws agree with the Constitution. The Supreme Court can "check" the other branches of government if it decides a law doesn't agree with the Constitution.

Practice

Look at the article again. Then complete the sentences. Circle *a*, *b*, or *c*.

1. The system of "checks and balances" means that _____.
   a. each of the three parts of the federal government limit the power of the other two
   b. the three parts of the federal government don't have power
   c. the federal government and state governments have the same amount of power

2. The Bill of Rights explains the rights of _____.
   a. the federal government
   b. the states
   c. the American people

3. Congress is _____.
   a. the Senate and the House of Representatives
   b. the president and vice president
   c. the Senate and the Supreme Court

4. Before a bill becomes a law, _____ must sign it.
   a. Congress   b. the Senate   c. the president

5. _____ can override a President's veto.
   a. Congress   b. The Supreme Court   c. The vice president

6. The _____ is Commander-in-Chief of the military.
   a. Secretary of Defense   b. president   c. vice president

7. _____ is the leader of the Senate.
   a. The president   b. The vice president   c. Congress

8. There are nine judges _____.
   a. in Congress   b. in the Executive Branch   c. on the Supreme Court

9. _____ can decide that a law doesn't agree with the Constitution.
   a. The Supreme Court   b. The president   c. Congress

Make It Yours

GROUPS OF 3. **Answer these questions about the U.S. government. If you don't know some answers, you can look online or ask another group.**

1. Who is the president? _____

2. Who is the vice president? _____

3. Who are the senators from your state? _____
   and _____

4. How many representatives does your state have? _____

5. Who is the representative of your district? _____

Learn

Note	Dial 911 if you see a crime while it's happening. If a crime has already happened, call your local police department. Sometimes you can report a crime over the phone, or sometimes an officer will come to you to file a report. In some cities, you can file a police report online.

A   **Match the pictures and the sentences.**

a.    b.    c.    d.

_____ 1. The robber put the wallet in his pocket.

_____ 2. The robber stole the woman's wallet from her purse.

_____ 3. The woman reported the crime to the police.

_____ 4. The woman saw that her wallet was missing.

B   **Look at the pictures again. Complete the sentences. Circle the correct words.**

1. The wallet was in the woman's **purse** / **pocket.**

2. The robber is a **man / woman.**

3. The man stole something. He **took / gave** something that doesn't belong to him without permission.

4. Now the man has the woman's **pocket / wallet.** It's in his **purse / pocket.**

5. The woman's wallet is missing. She **has / doesn't have** her wallet.

6. The woman reported the crime. She **listened to / told** the police officer.

Practice

1. **PD:** Police department.
   Meg: I'm calling to report a crime.
   PD: OK. Please describe what happened.
   Meg: Well, at about seven o'clock I was walking on Broad Street. Suddenly a man ran up behind me. He told me to give him my purse. I told him I didn't have any cash, but he took my purse anyway. Then he ran away toward Central Bus Station. My wallet was in my purse with my driver's license and all my credit cards! Luckily he didn't take my cell phone since that was in my pocket.
   PD: OK. You'll need to file a report, so I need some more information from you. . . .

2. **PD:** Police department.
   Tim: I need to report a crime.
   PD: OK. Tell me what happened.
   Tim: Well, at about eight o'clock I parked my car in the parking lot behind Central Shopping Mart and went into the store. I came back to my car a few minutes later, and I saw the window on the driver's side was broken. I think a robber threw something heavy to break the window. Now my stereo is missing. And the robber also stole ten CDs.
   PD: OK. You'll need to file a police report. You can come to the police station or I can send an officer to you. . . .

B **Read the conversations again. Read the sentences. Circle _T_ for _True_ or _F_ for _False_.**

1.	Meg said she didn't have any money.	(T)	F
2.	A robber stole Meg's purse and wallet.	T	F
3.	The robber took Meg's credit cards.	T	F
4.	The robber didn't steal Meg's cell phone because it wasn't in her purse.	T	F
5.	Meg called the police to report the crime.	T	F
6.	Tim was parking his car when the crime happened.	T	F
7.	Tim saw the robber.	T	F
8.	A robber stole Tim's stereo.	T	F
9.	Now Tim's car is missing.	T	F
10.	Tim can go to the police station to file the report.	T	F

Make It Yours

PAIRS. **Read the situations. Should you call 911 or the local police department? Explain your answers.**

1. You see someone break a window of your neighbor's house and go inside.
2. You were shopping, and you had your wallet in your pocket. When you get home, you see that your wallet is missing.

Unit 9 Test

Before you take the test

A B C D Use the answer sheet for Unit 9 on page 237.

1. Print your name.
2. Print your teacher's name.
3. Write your student identification number, and bubble in the information below the boxes.
4. Write the test date and bubble in the information.
5. Write your class number and bubble in the information.

 Listening I [Tracks 48–51]

You will hear a conversation. Then you will hear a question about the conversation. What is the correct answer: A, B, or C?

1. A. He celebrated with his family.

   B. He watched fireworks.

   C. He didn't celebrate the holiday.

2. A. holidays in the United States

   B. the three parts of the U.S. government

   C. the president of the United States

3. A. There was a crime.

   B. A police officer stopped a crime.

   C. A robber stole some money.

Listening II [Tracks 52–55]

Listen to the first part of the conversation. What should the person say next: A, B, or C?

4. A. Yes. I'm going to have a picnic.

B. Yes. It's Memorial Day.

C. Yes. It's the last Monday in May.

5. A. Thanksgiving is in November.

B. Yes. I celebrate Thanksgiving.

C. I have a big dinner with my family.

6. A. Yes. A man stole my wallet.

B. No. I didn't have money in my wallet.

C. Yes. My cell phone was in my purse.

Listening III [Tracks 56–59]

Listen. Questions 7, 8, and 9 are on the audio CD.

Reading

Read. What is the correct answer? A, B, C or D?

For many Americans, summer is a time for vacations. In the United States, we celebrate three holidays each summer.

Memorial Day is the last Monday in May. On this holiday, Americans honor people in the military who have died in wars. Many people also think of this day as the start of summer.

July 4, or Independence Day, is a very important holiday in the United States. On this day, Americans celebrate the United States' independence from Great Britain. Many people watch parades and have picnics to celebrate this holiday. At night, people usually watch fireworks.

Labor Day is the first Monday in September. On this day, Americans honor all workers. Many schools start after this day, so Labor Day is often considered the unofficial end of summer.

---

10. What does the information explain?

   A. good places for summer vacations

   B. summer holidays in the United States

   C. celebrations in different countries

   D. military holidays in the United States

11. Which holidays are NOT on the same date every year?

   A. Independence Day and Memorial Day

   B. Memorial Day and Labor Day

   C. Labor Day and Independence Day

   D. July 4 and Labor Day

The Federal Government

The U.S. Constitution was written in 1789. It is the highest law of the United States, and it explains how the federal government works.

The Constitution separates the powers of the federal government into three parts, or branches. These are the legislative branch, the executive branch, and the judicial branch. The legislative branch is made up of the Senate and the House of Representatives. The executive branch includes the president, the vice president, and the cabinet: other officials who are chosen by the president. The judicial branch includes the Supreme Court and all the federal courts.

The Constitution explains how the three branches of government work together. Each branch has different powers, and each one makes sure that no other branch has too much power or control. This system is called "checks and balances."

---

12. What does this reading explain?

    A. why the Constitution was written

    B. the three parts of the federal government

    C. the parts of the legislative branch

    D. the powers of the executive branch

13. What does the system of "checks and balances" do?

    A. makes sure the Constitution is the highest law of the United States

    B. makes sure the president has the most control

    C. makes sure the Supreme Court checks the power of other courts

    D. makes sure no part of the government has too much control

Ginny was shopping for a new computer at Great Buys. While she was there, she saw a man take a wallet out of a woman's purse. The man quickly ran out the door with the woman's wallet.

Ginny immediately told a salesperson what she had seen, and the salesperson called the police. The officers arrived quickly. They talked with Ginny and Alice, the woman whose wallet was taken. Ginny told them how the man took the wallet from Alice's purse and put it in his pocket. Alice told the officers what was in her wallet. The police wrote down everything to make a report.

14. What happened at Great Buys?

    A. A man took Ginny's purse.

    B. A man stole a computer from the store.

    C. A man stole a woman's wallet.

    D. A man took something from the salesperson.

15. What happened after the officers arrived?

    A. The robber ran out of the store.

    B. Ginny and Alice talked to the police.

    C. The police found Alice's wallet.

    D. The salesperson wrote a report.

Unit 10 Health

Learn

 60 Look at the diagram. Listen, read, and repeat.

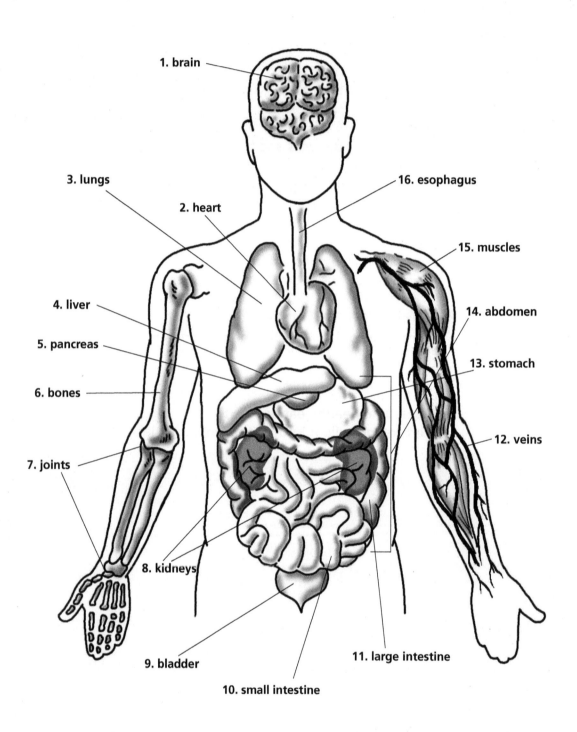

1. brain
3. lungs
2. heart
4. liver
5. pancreas
6. bones
7. joints
8. kidneys
9. bladder
10. small intestine
11. large intestine
16. esophagus
15. muscles
14. abdomen
13. stomach
12. veins

Practice

A   *PAIRS.* **Complete the sentences. Use the names of the parts of the body in the boxes. Use a dictionary if necessary.**

brain	heart	lungs	veins

1. Your _____ controls how you think, feel, and move.

2. You breathe with your _____.

3. Your _____ pushes blood through your body

4. Your _____ carry blood from other parts of the body back to your heart.

esophagus	liver	small intestine	stomach

5. Digestion, or breaking food down so your body can use it, starts in your mouth when you chew food. The food moves from your mouth down through your

   _____.

6. Then digestion continues in your _____.

7. Your body continues to digest food in your _____ after it goes through your stomach.

8. Your _____ cleans your blood and makes a liquid that helps you digest fats.

bladder	kidneys	large intestine	pancreas

9. Your _____ clean your blood and make liquid waste (urine).

10. Your _____ holds liquid waste (urine) until it goes out of the body.

11. Your _____ changes food that your body can't use into solid waste (feces).

12. Your _____ makes insulin, a liquid that helps your body use the food you eat.

abdomen	bones	joint	muscles

13. Your _____ are hard and support your body.

14. A _____ is where two bones meet. It allows that part of your body to bend.

15. Your _____ allow your body to move.

16. Your _____ is the front part of your body between your chest and your legs.

B   *GROUPS OF 4.* **Pairs compare answers with another pair.**

Lesson 2   Diseases and Medical Conditions

Learn

A   🔘 **61** **Listen and repeat the diseases and medical conditions.**

cancer	AIDS	depression
tuberculosis (TB)	arthritis	heart disease
asthma	diabetes	pneumonia
hepatitis	hypertension	the flu
allergies	high cholesterol	

Childhood Diseases

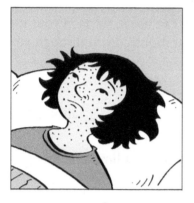

measles

mumps

chicken pox

You can get these diseases anytime in life, but they're most common in children.

B   *PAIRS.* **Complete the chart. Write each disease or medical condition under the part of the body it affects. Use a dictionary if necessary.**

arthritis	diabetes	hepatitis	hypertension	tuberculosis (TB)
asthma	heart disease	high cholesterol	pneumonia	

heart	joints	liver	lungs	pancreas
1.	4.	5.	6.	9.
2.			7.	
3.			8.	

Practice

A Match the diseases and medical conditions with their descriptions.

___e___ 1. allergy

_____ 2. cancer

_____ 3. tuberculosis (TB)

_____ 4. hepatitis

_____ 5. asthma

_____ 6. hypertension

_____ 7. the flu

a. a serious liver disease that makes the skin yellow

b. a serious, contagious disease caused by an infection, usually in the lungs

c. a condition, often caused by allergies, that makes it difficult to breathe

d. high blood pressure

e. a condition that makes you sick when you eat, touch, or breathe a particular thing

f. a common illness that is like a cold but more serious

g. a serious disease that makes tumors grow in the body

B Match the diseases and medical conditions with their descriptions.

___d___ 1. diabetes

_____ 2. high cholesterol

_____ 3. pneumonia

_____ 4. depression

_____ 5. heart disease

_____ 6. AIDS

_____ 7. arthritis

a. a mental condition that makes you feel sad and without energy a lot of the time

b. a serious illness caused by an infection of the lungs that makes it difficult to breathe

c. a disease that makes it impossible for the body to fight infections; caused by a virus, or type of germ, called HIV

d. a disease in which there's too much sugar in the blood

e. a disease that stops the heart from working correctly

f. a condition that causes the joints to become painful and hard to move

g. a condition in which there's too much fat in the blood

Make It Yours

GROUPS OF 3. **What other diseases or medical conditions do you know of? What parts of the body do they affect?**

Learn

A **Complete the sentences. Use the words in the box.**

| currently | health insurance | physician | record | Treatment |

1. When you have _____, you pay a company a certain amount of money, usually every month. Then, if you need to see a doctor or go to the hospital, the company pays all or part of the costs.

2. Something that is happening _____ is happening now.

3. A _____ is a doctor.

4. When you _____ information, you write it down so it can be looked at in the future.

5. _____ is something that is done to make a sick person better.

B **Read the medical history form.**

NEW PATIENT INFORMATION

Please write all information clearly.

First name: Bao Yu   Last name: Cheng

Date of birth (mm/dd/yy) 07 / 02 / 80

Insurance company: Healthy Sure   Group number: 0000 - 1286 - 4429

Are you currently under the care of a physician for any condition?   ✓ yes   no

Name of doctor: Dr. Gray   Reason: allergies and asthma

Please list all medications you are currently taking.   Breathe Max

Are you allergic to any medications?   ✓ yes   no   Which?   penicillin

Please use a ✓ to record any medical conditions that you or any family members have or had.

	you	family member		you	family member
allergies	✓	✓	heart disease		
asthma	✓		hepatitis		
cancer			hypertension		✓
diabetes		✓	high cholesterol		✓
tuberculosis (TB)			HIV/AIDS		

Please explain. I'm allergic to dust, cats, and dogs. I also have asthma. My father has allergies and diabetes. My mother has hypertension and high cholesterol.

Have you ever received treatment for a mental condition?   ✓ yes   no

Please explain. From Aug. 2007 to Aug. 2008 I saw a doctor for depression.

Practice

Look at the medical history form in Learn again. Read the sentences.
Circle *T* for *True* or *F* for *False*.

1. The doctor records information on this form. T (F)
2. Bao Yu has health insurance. T F
3. Bao Yu currently receives treatment from Dr. Gray for allergies. T F
4. Bao Yu is currently taking penicillin. T F
5. Bao Yu doesn't have any history of medical conditions. T F
6. No one in Bao Yu's family has a history of cancer. T F
7. Bao Yu has hypertension. T F
8. Bao Yu currently receives treatment for depression. T F

Make It Yours

Fill out the medical history form with your own information. You can use real or made-up information.

NEW PATIENT INFORMATION

Please write all information clearly.

First name: Last name:

Date of birth (mm/dd/yy)

Insurance company: Group number:

Are you currently under the care of a physician for any condition?   yes   no
Name of doctor: Reason:

Please list all medications you are currently taking.
Are you allergic to any medications?   yes   no   Which?

Please use a ✓ to record any medical conditions that you or any family members have or had.

	you	family member		you	family member
allergies			heart disease		
asthma			hepatitis		
cancer			hypertension		
diabetes			high cholesterol		
tuberculosis (TB)			HIV/AIDS		

Please explain.

Have you ever received treatment for a mental condition?   yes   no
Please explain.

BONUS *GROUPS OF 3.* **Why do doctors ask about the medical history of patients' family members? What are some diseases that are common in families?**

Learn

> **Note** A symptom *is a problem with your body that shows you have a certain disease or medical condition.*

A **62** **Look at the pictures of symptoms and listen. Number the pictures in the order in which you hear them.**

_____ I've been having trouble sleeping.

_____ I have a burning feeling in my chest.

_____ I've been losing weight.

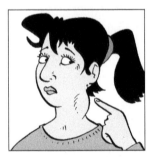

_____ My glands are swollen.

_____ My vision is blurry.

_____ I'm having difficulty breathing.

_____ I have pain in my abdomen.

_____ I feel exhausted.

_____ My muscles ache.

_____ I'm nauseous.

B *PAIRS.* **Check your answers.**

Practice

A 🎵 63 **Listen and read the conversation between a doctor and his first patient. Then practice with a partner.**

Doctor: What seems to be the matter?
Patient: I've been <u>feeling exhausted</u>, and I don't know why. Also, <u>my muscles ache</u>.
Doctor: I see. How long has this been going on?
Patient: <u>For a few weeks</u>.

B *PAIRS.* **Create three new conversations. Use the information in the box. Switch roles.**

1. losing weight / my glands are swollen / for about a month
2. having difficulty breathing / I've been getting headaches / for a few days
3. feeling nauseous / I've been having a burning feeling in my chest / since Monday

C 🎵 64 **Listen and read the conversation between the doctor and his second patient. Then practice with a partner.**

Doctor: So, what's the problem?
Patient: Sometimes <u>I have a burning feeling in my chest</u>.
Doctor: How often does this happen?
Patient: <u>Three or four times a week</u>.

D *PAIRS.* **Create three new conversations. Use the information in the box. Switch roles.**

1. my vision is blurry / a couple of times a week
2. I have trouble sleeping / maybe five or six times a month
3. I have pain in my abdomen / a few times a week, usually after I eat

Listen

 65 **Listen to each question. What is the correct answer? Circle *a* or *b*.**

1. **a.** Every day.   **b.** I have a burning feeling in my chest.
2. **a.** My vision is blurry.   **b.** I don't have any symptoms.
3. **a.** two or three times a week   **b.** for two or three days
4. **a.** for about four days   **b.** about three or four times a week

BONUS *PAIRS.* **Have you or has anyone you know been to a doctor in the United States? How was the experience similar to or different from going to the doctor in your country? Share your experiences.**

Learn

Note

Immunizations *help keep people safe from certain diseases. When people receive immunizations, they are given a* vaccine, *or a very small amount of a disease. This causes the body to build up* immunity, *or protection, to the disease.*

immunization by injection

oral immunization

In the United States, children must get certain doses, *or amounts, of specific vaccines before they are allowed to go to school. When a child receives an immunization, the doctor gives the child's parent a* record, *or information written on a special card, of the immunization. It is the responsibility of parents to provide these immunization records to their children's schools.*

Read the information about school immunization requirements.

Hayes Public School District

Preparing Your Child for Kindergarten Registration

Before you register your child for kindergarten in the Hayes Public School District, you must provide a copy of your child's immunization record, including the dates when your child received the following required vaccines:

- 5 doses of DTP (diphtheria, pertussis, tetanus)
- 4 doses of IPV (polio)
- 3 doses of Hepatitis B
- 2 doses of MMR (measles, mumps, rubella)
- 1 dose of Hib (Haemophilus influenzae type b)
- 1 dose of chicken pox (or varicella) or disease history*

It's your responsibility! Make sure your child is ready for school.

- Check your child's immunization records to make sure all the required vaccines have been given.
- If your child still needs any immunizations, make an appointment now with your child's physician. Sometimes you can also get immunizations at your county health department.

*Parents must provide an immunization record or a doctor's record of the child's having certain diseases.

Practice

A **Look at the information on school immunization requirements again. Complete the sentences. Circle the correct words.**

1. People receive immunizations **when they are sick / to protect them from diseases**.

2. An immunization record shows the vaccines a child **needs / has received**.

3. Parents must show their child's immunization records to the **doctor / school**.

4. The information gives the immunization requirements for **all students / kindergarten students** in the Hayes Public School District.

5. **Physicians / Parents** give immunizations.

6. Children can get immunizations at **school / the county health department**.

7. **Doctors / Parents** must make sure a child has received all the required immunizations.

8. A child's disease history shows if a child **had / received** immunization against a disease.

B **Look at the information on school immunization requirements again. Read the sentences. Circle T for True or F for False.**

1. Students must have five doses of DTP.   **(T) F**

2. IPV protects against polio.   **T F**

3. Children who have had the mumps don't need MMR immunizations.   **T F**

4. Students are required to have three doses of Hib.   **T F**

C **Look at the information about school immunization requirements again. Answer the questions.**

Amelia is going to enter kindergarten in the Hayes Public School District. She hasn't been immunized against chicken pox, but she had the disease last year. Does she have to get the chicken pox vaccine? Why or why not? If she doesn't get the vaccine, what do her parents have to show the school?

_____

_____

_____

BONUS **Find out where children can get immunizations in your area. (Hint: Immunizations are often given at clinics, hospitals, pharmacies, and county or state health departments.) Share your information with the class.**

Learn

 A   **Read the information in the article.**

Good Habits, Good Health

Your everyday habits are very important to your health.

Eat well. A healthy diet will help you control your weight. It can prevent or control many conditions and diseases, such as heart disease, hypertension, cancer, and diabetes. Start your day with a good breakfast. Eat only when you are hungry, and chew your food well.

Exercise. Exercise is necessary for good health. It can help reduce stress, control your weight, prevent depression, and keep your blood pressure and cholesterol at healthy levels. You should do moderate activity, such as walking, riding a bike, working in the yard, or dancing for 30–60 minutes a day at least four times a week. Choose activities that you enjoy or that you can do as part of your regular schedule, and make them part of your life.

Drink water. Your body needs water. A healthy adult needs at least eight to ten 8-oz. glasses of water each day.

Get enough sleep. Most people need seven to nine hours of sleep a night. Many people don't get enough sleep, and if this continues over time, it can lead to illness. It's best for your body if you go to bed and get up at the same time every day.

Reduce stress. Stress can make us feel nervous and worried. In response, we tense, or tighten, our muscles. Stress can create problems in our bodies. People with a lot of stress are more likely to have health problems, including headaches, depression, high blood pressure, heart disease, and even cancer. It's important to reduce stress. One of the best ways is to exercise regularly. Also, make time for activities you enjoy. And it's important to relax: Sit or lie quietly, and pay attention to your body. Follow your breath as it goes in and out. Then start to breathe more deeply and more slowly. Notice how this relaxes the body and calms the mind.

Quit smoking. Smoking can cause high blood pressure, heart disease, and cancer. Quitting is one of the best things you can do for your health.

Take care of your teeth. Brush your teeth twice a day, and use dental floss every day. Avoid foods that are high in sugar. Get your teeth cleaned by a dentist twice a year.

Visit your doctor. Consult a doctor if you have symptoms or a health problem that persists. In addition, it's a good idea to have a check-up once every few years even if you don't have symptoms. Many times your physician can discover diseases and conditions early, and you can control or treat them before they become serious.

B **Match the words with their definitions.**

<u>b</u> 1. habit   a. not too much, not too little

____ 2. stress   b. something you do regularly, and usually without thinking

____ 3. prevent   c. continue to exist or happen

____ 4. moderate   d. stay away from someone or something

____ 5. avoid   e. strong feelings of nervousness and worry, muscle tightness, and poor breathing

____ 6. consult

____ 7. persist   f. stop something from happening

g. to ask or look for advice or information from someone

Practice

Read the article again. Complete the sentences. Circle *a*, *b*, or *c*.

1. The article says that exercise _____.

   a. is a treatment for many diseases   **b.** is a moderate habit   **c.** can prevent depression

2. Adults should have _____ per day.

   a. less than seven hours of sleep   **b.** two hours of exercise   **c.** eight to ten glasses of water

3. If you don't get enough sleep, you might _____.

   a. get sick   **b.** get up too early   **c.** go to bed at the same time every day

4. The article says you should _____ to reduce stress.

   a. visit your doctor   **b.** quit smoking   **c.** exercise

5. The article says you shouldn't _____.

   a. smoke   **b.** do activities you enjoy   **c.** eat breakfast

6. You should _____ two times every day.

   a. brush your teeth   **b.** use dental floss   **c.** drink water

7. If a medical problem is discovered early, it is easier to _____.

   a. get a checkup   **b.** treat the problem   **c.** consult a doctor

Make It Yours

GROUPS OF 3. **What healthy habits do you have? How could you improve your health? Talk about your habits and your health.**

Learn

Read the article. Then complete the sentences. Use the words in the box.

Good Food Choices

Your body needs a variety of foods. Make good choices about every food you eat.

Fruits and Vegetables: It's very important to eat lots of fresh fruits and vegetables. Eat as many different colors as possible since each color represents different vitamins.

Grains: Prefer whole grains, such as brown rice, whole wheat bread, and oatmeal to refined ones, such as white rice and white bread. (When grains are refined, they lose most of their nutrients and vitamins.) Look for the words "whole grain" on food labels.

Protein: Include protein such as fish, eggs, poultry, or lean meat in your diet. Or combine grains and beans for vegetarian protein. Dry beans, nuts, and seeds are vegetables, but they have high amounts of protein, too.

Dairy: Choose fat-free or low-fat milk, yogurt, and cheese. Be careful of large amounts of sugar in some dairy products, such as yogurt and ice cream.

Fats: Certain oils, such as olive oil, sesame oil, and canola oil, are good for you and should be a part of your diet. But don't eat a lot of fats that come from animal sources (like butter or lard). Trans fats, often listed in ingredients as partially hydrogenated oils, are dangerous and should be avoided. Also, avoid fried foods.

Sugar: Many foods, such as fruit and even vegetables, have natural sugar. For most people, sugar in this form is fine. But try to avoid foods that have added sugar, such as soda, fruit drinks, candy, and other desserts. Read the list of ingredients on foods to help identify how much added sugar they contain. Some other names for sugar include cane juice, corn sweetener, corn syrup, dextrose, fructose, glucose, sucrose, fruit juice concentrate, syrup, and honey.

Salt: Many processed, or already prepared, foods contain a lot of salt. Look for salt on ingredients lists — sometimes it's also called sodium. Try to avoid eating too much salt. It can cause problems for people with high blood pressure.

dairy	grains	lean	poultry

1. Meat from birds, such as chicken, duck, and turkey, is called _____ *poultry* _____.

2. Meat without a lot of fat is _____.

3. The seeds of plants, such as corn, wheat, or rice, are called _____.

4. Foods made from milk are called _____ products.

Practice

A   Look at the article again. Read the sentences. Circle *T* for *True* or *F* for *False*.

1. Different vegetables have different vitamins. (T) F
2. White rice has more nutrients and vitamins than brown rice. T F
3. Eggs and meat are types of protein. T F
4. You can get protein from seeds and nuts. T F
5. Some dairy products have a lot of sugar. T F
6. You should try not to eat any oil. T F
7. Hydrogenated oil isn't good for you. T F
8. Dextrose is a kind of sugar. T F

B   Look at the article again. Read the pairs of foods. For each pair, circle the food that is healthier.

1. butter / olive oil
2. fruit / fruit drink
3. whole wheat bread / white bread
4. canola oil / lard

Make It Yours

PAIRS. Look at the labels from two cereal boxes. Complete the chart. Record the grains, fats, and sugars in each cereal. Which cereal do you think is healthier? Explain your answer.

Wholey O's Cereal

Ingredients: whole grain oats, whole grain wheat, sugar, honey, canola oil, almonds, salt

Nutty Oat Crunch Cereal

Ingredients: oats, corn syrup, wheat, almonds, partially hydrogenated palm oil, high-fructose corn syrup, salt

	grains	fats	sugars
Wholey O's Cereal			
Nutty Oat Crunch Cereal			

Unit 10 Test

Listening I [Tracks 66–69]

You will hear a conversation. Then you will hear a question about the conversation. What is the correct answer: A, B, or C?

1. Where is the boy's problem?

   A. in his lungs

   B. in his liver

   C. in his joints

2. What will the doctor probably check?

   A. the woman's abdomen

   B. the woman's bones

   C. the woman's muscles

3. What condition does the woman probably have?

   A. chicken pox

   B. depression

   C. diabetes

Listening II [Tracks 70–73]

Listen. Questions 4, 5, and 6 are on the audio CD.

Reading

Read. What is the correct answer: A, B, C, or D?

What's in Your Drink?

The label on your drink says *fruit*, but is the drink healthy? Many fruit drinks have a lot of added sugar, which isn't good for your body. Before you buy any fruit drink, read the list of ingredients. Look for added sugar. And be careful—sometimes companies use different kinds of sugar, such as cane juice, glucose, and corn syrup. Sugar is sugar! Make smart choices about what you drink.

---

7. What does the article explain?

    A. why sugar is bad for your body

    B. how to find out if a drink has added sugar

    C. the names of some drinks without added sugar

    D. where to buy drinks without added sugar

8. What is glucose?

    A. a fruit

    B. a fruit drink

    C. a list of ingredients

    D. a type of sugar

Medical History Form

Write all information clearly.

First name: _____Luis_____   Last name: _____Camacho_____

Date of birth (mm/dd/yy) _05/30/73_

Insurance company: _Atlanticare Health_   Group number: _000-222-1110_

Are you currently under the care of a physician for any condition ☑ yes ☐ no

Name of doctor: _____Dr. H. Ramirez_____   Reason: _____asthma_____

Please list all medications you are currently taking. _____Breathegen_____

Do you have any allergies to medications? ☑ yes ☐ no Which? _codeine_

Record any medical conditions that you or any family members have or had.

	you	family member		you	family member
allergies	☐	☐	heart disease	☐	☑
asthma	☑	☐	hepatitis	☐	☐
cancer	☐	☐	hypertension	☐	☑
diabetes	☐	☑	high cholesterol	☑	☐
tuberculosis (TB)	☐	☐	HIV/AIDS	☐	☐

Please explain. _I have asthma and high cholesterol. My mother has diabetes._
My father has heart disease and hypertension.

Have you ever received treatment for a mental condition? ☑ yes ☐ no

Please explain. _I was treated for depression from March to November of 2007._

---

9. Why is Luis receiving medical treatment now?

    A. He has asthma.

    B. He has allergies.

    C. He has diabetes.

    D. He is depressed.

10. Which medicine is Luis allergic to?

    A. asthma

    B. Breathegen

    C. codeine

    D. allergies

Truman Avenue Elementary School

Dear ___Mr. and Mrs. Whitman___ ,

Your child's immunization records are not complete.
Please provide the school with the immunization record
for ___Hib (Haemophilus influenza type b)___ for your child,
___Marcus Whitman___ .

If your child has been immunized, please bring or send
the immunization record to the school office. If your child
has not been immunized, you must make an appointment
with your child's doctor to get the immunization. We must
receive the record by September 3, 2010, or your child will
not be permitted to attend school.

Sincerely,

Caroline Bower

Caroline Bower, RN
School Nurse

---

11. What does the letter say?

 A. Marcus has the disease Hib.

 B. Marcus got Hib vaccine.

 C. The school needs Marcus's immunization record for Hib.

 D. The school will give Marcus the Hib vaccine.

12. What do Marcus's parents need to do by September 3, 2010?

 A. call the school office

 B. take Marcus to school

 C. make an appointment with the doctor

 D. bring or send the immunization record to the school office

Sada works very long hours. She is usually very healthy, but a few weeks ago she started to feel sick. She was having difficulty breathing, and she felt exhausted.

She went to see Dr. Patel. The doctor looked at her medical history and asked about her symptoms. He also asked about Sada's daily life, including her job and things she did for fun.

The doctor didn't give Sada any medicine, but he gave her some instructions. He said Sada had to reduce her stress because it was making her sick. Dr. Patel said Sada needed to get more exercise and to relax. He said these things would help reduce Sada's stress and make her feel better.

13. Why did Sada go to the doctor?

  A. She was very healthy.

  B. She wanted to relax.

  C. She couldn't breathe well, and she felt very tired.

  D. She needed some medicine and instructions.

14. What were Dr. Patel's instructions?

  A. Take medicine.

  B. Sleep more.

  C. Get more exercise.

  D. Go to the doctor more often.

Unit 11 Getting a Job

Lesson 1 — **Looking for a Job**
- Identify ways to find a job
- Use the Internet to look for a job

Lesson 2 — **Applying for Jobs**
- Understand job ads
- Ask about job requirements, duties, and application procedures

Lesson 3 — **Job Applications**
- Complete a job application

Lesson 4 — **Job Interviews**
- Demonstrate appropriate job interview behavior
- Respond to an interviewer's questions
- Ask appropriate questions at a job interview

Lesson 1 — Looking for a Job

Note *When you* hire *someone, you agree to pay the person to do a job.* Help wanted *or* job opening *means that a person or company wants to hire a worker or workers.*

Learn

Look at the pictures. Read about ways to look for a job.

Businesses sometimes put ads in the classified section of the newspaper when they need workers.

Sometimes store owners and business owners advertise job openings with signs in their windows.

Individuals and some businesses put up signs around the community when they're looking for workers. Look for these signs at places such as libraries, supermarkets, and schools.

There are many Internet websites that can help you find a job. If you know a website's address, such as www.jobfindnow.com, type it in the address box at the top of the webpage.

Make It Yours

GROUPS OF 3. **How have you found jobs in the past? Talk about your experiences.**

Learn

Read about another way to use the Internet to look for jobs.

If you don't have a specific website address, you can use a search engine, or a website that helps you find information on the Internet. Google and Yahoo are examples of search engines. To use a search engine, follow these steps:

1. Type the address for a search engine in the address box.

2. Hit *enter* or *return* on your keyboard.

3. Type one or more keywords. A keyword is a word you want the computer to look for on the Internet. For example, if you're looking for a job in a restaurant in Chicago, you might type *job restaurant Chicago*.

4. Click on *search*. You can also hit *enter* or *return*.

5. Look at the list of websites.

6. Click on a website you're interested in seeing.

7. Try different keywords to find more information.

BONUS Think of a job you might be interested in. Use a search engine to find jobs in your area. Use keywords like the name of the job and the name of your city. Record any websites you find.

Lesson 2   Applying for Jobs

Learn

A   *PAIRS.* **Read the job ads. Then write the words that match the meanings below.**

AUTO MECHANIC

Full-time, Monday–Saturday,
overtime available
$15 an hour, excellent benefits
minimum 1 year experience required
bilingual preferred
references required
Apply in person
at Fix-It Mechanics Shop.
Ask for manager.

Teacher's Assistant

Part-time, Monday–Friday,
no overtime
$10 an hour, no benefits
experience a plus
excellent references required
Call Gina for appointment,
305-555-4774.

---

a plus	bilingual	in person	minimum	part-time	reference
apply	experience	manager	overtime	preferred	required
benefits	full-time				

___benefits___   1. advantages you get from your job, such as health insurance, training, vacation days, and paid sick days

_____   2. time that you work at your job, usually for extra pay, in addition to your usual working hours

_____   3. working for the number of hours a week that people usually work (usually 35–40 hours a week in the United States)

_____   4. smallest number or amount it's possible or OK to have

_____   5. knowledge or skill you get from doing a job

_____   6. necessary

_____   7. can speak two languages

_____   8. good, but not necessary (Note: there are two words with this meaning.)

_____

_____   9. a person who recommends you for a job

_____   10. officially ask to be considered for a job opening

_____   11. go somewhere to do something instead of calling or sending an email

_____   12. person who directs the work of a business or organization

_____   13. working for only part of each day or week

B Look at the ads on page 178 again. Answer the questions.

1. Is it necessary to be bilingual for the auto mechanic job? _____ *no* _____

2. How do you apply for the auto mechanic job? _____

3. Do you need experience for the teacher's assistant job? _____

4. What do you need to have for the teacher's assistant job? _____

C Compare the job ads below with the ads on page 178. What do the abbreviations mean? Write the words.

Medical Assistant

FT
$13/hr., exc. bens.
min. 1 yr. exp. req.
biling. pref.
refs. req.
Dr. Raul Sanchez for appt.
201-555-0394

SECURITY GUARD

PT, Sat.-Sun., some OT
$10/hr., no bens.
exp. a +, refs. req.
Apply in prsn.
Ask for mgr.
Sanford Security
2422 W 20 St.

1. FT _____	7. exp. _____	13. PT _____
2. hr. _____	8. req. _____	14. OT _____
3. exc. _____	9. biling. _____	15. a + _____
4. bens. _____	10. pref. _____	16. prsn. _____
5. min. _____	11. refs. _____	17. mgr. _____
6. yr. _____	12. appt. _____	

Practice

Look at the job ads in Exercise C again. Read the sentences. Check *Medical Assistant, Security Guard,* or *Both*.

	Medical Assistant	Security Guard	Both
1. This job includes benefits.	☑	❏	❏
2. Extra hours are available for this job.	❏	❏	❏
3. Experience is needed for this job.	❏	❏	❏
4. You need references for this job.	❏	❏	❏

Listen

74   **Listen. Which sentence is correct? Circle *a*, *b*, or *c*.**

1. **a.** Frank works full-time.

    b. Frank works part-time.

    c. Frank works overtime.

2. **a.** Call Rita to apply for the job.

    b. Go to the restaurant to apply for the job.

    c. Talk to a worker to apply for the job.

3. **a.** Experience is a plus.

    b. Experience is required.

    c. They prefer a person without experience.

4. **a.** The job starts every day at 12:00.

    b. You have to work 12 hours a day for this job.

    c. You'll get paid $12 an hour for this job.

5. **a.** Marta wants a job at The Super Market.

    b. Marta works at The Super Market.

    c. Marta has experience working at The Super Market.

6. **a.** Talk to Don to apply for the job.

    b. Don got the job.

    c. Don wants to apply for the job.

Make It Yours

A   **Create an ad for the job you have or a job you want. Include information about the schedule, pay, benefits, and requirements. Give instructions on how to apply for the job. Use abbreviations. You can use made-up information.**

B   *PAIRS.* **Switch job ads. Look at your partner's job ad. Read the ad and explain it out loud.**

> **Example:**
> *Your job ad is for a plumber. The schedule is Monday through Thursday. . . .*

Learn

Note Before you apply for a job, you can ask about requirements for the job, the schedule, and duties, or things you have to do because they're part of the job.

 Miguel saw a job ad in the newspaper for a truck driver. He called to find out more about the job. Listen and read the conversation. Then practice with a partner.

A: Hello. <u>Joe Thompson</u>.

B: Hello. My name is <u>Miguel Santos</u>. I'm calling about the opening for a <u>truck driver</u>. I'd like to know more about the job.

A: Sure. What would you like to know?

B: Well, is experience required?

A: <u>No, it's not actually required, but it's preferred</u>.

B: OK. And what are the job duties?

A: They include <u>driving the truck and carrying heavy boxes</u>.

B: All right. What's the schedule?

A: <u>Monday through Saturday, 8:00–4:00</u>.

B: OK. And how do I apply?

A: You need to <u>apply in person</u>.

B: <u>OK. Can you give me the address</u>?

A: . . .

WANTED

Truck driver

F/T, good bens.

Start work immed.

Call Joe Thompson

at 420-555-2780.

Practice

PAIRS. ROLE PLAY. **Call about a job opening. Use your own names and the information in the boxes. Switch roles.**

- office assistant
- Yes, some experience is required.
- organizing files and making copies
- Monday through Friday, 8:30–5:30
- make an appointment. Can you come in tomorrow at 1:00?
- Yes, that would be fine.

- salesperson
- No, but experience is preferred.
- helping customers and using a cash register
- Saturday and Sunday, 1:00–9:00
- apply in person during store hours
- OK. And what are the store hours?

Learn

A Read the job application.

APPLICATION FOR EMPLOYMENT

Personal Information

Name: *Mei-Yu Huang*

Address: *822 Casitas Street, Apt. 4, San Francisco, CA 94123*   Phone: *415-555-6483*

Availability

Desired position: *housekeeping manager*   Available starting date: *10/12/09*

Are you available: ✓ full-time   part-time   overtime

✓ days   nights   ✓ weekends

Education (begin with present or last school)

School name and location: *Mission Adult School*

29838 Thompson Street, San Francisco, CA 94112

From: *Sept. 2008*   To: *present*   Graduated?   Yes ✓ No

School name and location: *Anderson High School*

7000 School Lane, San Francisco, CA 94114

From: *Sept. 2000*   To: *June 2004*   Graduated? ✓ Yes   No

Employment (begin with present or last job)

Employer: *Hotel Grand*   Address: *1875 Main Street, San Francisco, CA 94104*

Phone: *415-555-0111*   Position: *housekeeper*

From (Month/Year): *June 2006*   To (Month/Year): *Sept. 2008*

Duties: *clean rooms, make beds*   Supervisor's Name: *Margarita Lopez*

Reason for Leaving: *I left to study English full-time.*

Employer: *Congress Hotel*   Address: *201 Carter Avenue, San Francisco, CA 94104*

Phone: *415-555-2300*   Position: *housekeeper*

From (Month/Year): *June 2004*   To (Month/Year): *June 2006*

Duties: *clean rooms, make beds*   Supervisor's Name: *Karita Patel*

Reason for Leaving: *The job was part-time, and I needed a full-time position.*

Other Skills (languages, training, equipment, machines, etc.)

I speak Mandarin Chinese.

References (no family members)

Name	Phone number	Relationship	Years known
Carrie Banks	*415-555-4837*	*English teacher*	*2*
Margarita Lopez	*415-555-0157*	*supervisor (Hotel Grand)*	*3*
Karita Patel	*415-555-2877*	*supervisor (Congress Hotel)*	*4*

Signature: *Mei-Yu Huang*   Date: *10/7/09*

B   Look at the application again. Match the words and definitions.

_d_ 1. desired   a. job

____ 2. position   b. person who is in charge of something or someone, a boss

____ 3. present   c. ability to do something very well

____ 4. skill   d. wanted

____ 5. supervisor   e. happening or existing now

Practice

A   Look at the application again. Match the information with the correct section of the application.

_c_ 1. Mei-Yu's school   a. Personal Information

____ 2. Mei-Yu's job experience   b. Availability

____ 3. the day Mei-Yu can begin the job   c. Education

____ 4. people who can recommend Mei-Yu for the job   d. Employment

____ 5. Mei-Yu's home address   e. Other Skills

____ 6. other things Mei-Yu can do well   f. References

B   Look at the application again. Read the sentences. Circle *T* for *True* or *F* for *False*.

1. Mei-Yu is applying for the position of housekeeping manager.   (T) F

2. Mei-Yu can begin working on October 12.   T   F

3. Mei-Yu worked in Hotel Grand before the Congress Hotel.   T   F

4. Mei-Yu left her last job because she wanted to study English.   T   F

5. Kavita Patel was Mei-Yu's boss.   T   F

Make It Yours

A   GROUPS OF 3. **The "Other Skills" section of a job application is a place to write other abilities. Tell your group at least one skill you have.**

B   GROUPS OF 3. **Past or present bosses, co-workers, and teachers can be good references. Make sure you choose people who will say good things about you and your work. Tell your group the names of three people that you could use as references. Explain your relationship to each person.**

C Complete the application with your own information. You can use real or made-up information.

APPLICATION FOR EMPLOYMENT

Personal Information

Name:
Address: Phone:

Availability

Desired position: Available starting date:
Are you available: full time   part time   overtime
                        days   nights   weekends

Education (begin with present or last school)

School name and location:

From: To: Graduated?   Yes   No
School name and location:

From: To: Graduated?   Yes   No

Employment (begin with present or last job)

Employer: Address:
Phone: Position:
From (Month/Year):   To (Month/Year):
Duties: Supervisor's Name:
Reason for Leaving:

Employer: Address:
Phone: Position:
From (Month/Year):   To (Month/Year):
Duties: Supervisor's Name:
Reason for Leaving:

Other Skills (languages, training, equipment, machines, etc.)

References (no family members)

Name   Phone number   Relationship   Years known

Signature: Date:

Learn

Match the pictures to the sentences.

1. _d_   2. ____   3. ____   4. ____

5. ____   6. ____   7. ____

a. Shake hands, look at the interviewer, smile, and introduce yourself.
b. Make eye contact as you talk. Sit up straight and don't move around a lot.
c. Throw away gum, food, or drink before the interview.
d. Look neat and dress professionally.
e. Arrive on time.
f. Thank the interviewer.
g. Turn off your cell phone before the interview.

Practice

Complete the sentences. Circle *should* or *shouldn't*.

1. You **should / shouldn't** wear jeans to an interview.

2. You **should / shouldn't** be five minutes late for an interview.

3. You **should / shouldn't** shake hands with the interviewer.

4. You **should / shouldn't** look at the interviewer while you're talking.

Make It Yours

CLASS. **Walk around the room and introduce yourself to at least five classmates. Give a strong handshake, make eye contact, and smile.**

Learn

Read some common interview questions and ideas about how to answer those questions. Always give honest answers, so use only those ideas that are true for your situation.

Question:	How to answer:
What kind of work experience do you have?	Talk about jobs you've had and the duties of those jobs.
Why do you want to leave your job?	Don't say bad things about the company or your boss. Talk about positive things that you want, such as • an opportunity to learn more. • a position with more responsibility. • a different schedule. • a job closer to home.
Do you have any experience with _____?	Say yes and give an example. Or say no and explain that you • want to learn and that you can learn quickly. • have other experience that might be useful.

Practice

 76 Listen and read part of a conversation at a job interview. Then practice with a partner.

A: What kind of work experience do you have?

B: I've been working at Good Foods grocery store for three years. My duties there include checking orders to make sure we receive the correct items and putting items on the shelves. Before that, I worked at a restaurant. I washed dishes there.

A: OK. And why do you want to leave your job now?

B: Some day I want to be a manager. I don't have that opportunity at my present job.

A: All right. Do you have any experience with computers?

B: Yes, I do. I use a computer to write emails and keep in touch with family and friends.

Make It Yours

Read the questions in the conversation again. On a separate piece of paper, write your own answers to the questions.

BONUS *PAIRS. ROLE PLAY.* **Practice an interview. Student A, you're interviewing for a job. Introduce yourself and answer the interviewer's questions. Student B, you're the interviewer. Ask the questions in the conversation in Practice. Switch roles.**

Learn

Read the information about asking questions at an interview.

> An interview lets employers see if you're a good person to work for them. But it also gives you the opportunity to learn about the employer. It's important to ask questions at a job interview.
> - Ask questions to learn about the employer and decide whether the position is right for you.
> - Ask questions to show the interviewer that you really are interested in the job.
> - It's better to wait until *after* you are offered the job to ask about pay and benefits.

Practice

 Listen and read the end of a job interview. Then practice with a partner.

A: Well, those are all of my questions. Do you have anything you'd like to ask me?

B: Yes, I have a few questions.

A: Sure. Go ahead.

B: Do you provide training to new employees?

A: Good question. Yes, we provide a three-day training session, which will explain everything you need to know.

B: That sounds good. What are the working hours?

A: 8:30 to 4:30.

B: And do people work overtime?

A: Overtime hours are available, but they're not required.

B: That's good. I can do some overtime. What's the start date for this position?

A: We need someone by the end of the month.

B: That would be very good for me. And could you tell me when you're going to decide?

A: We'll let you know our decision by Friday.

B: Great. It was a pleasure meeting you. Thank you very much for your time.

Make It Yours

PAIRS. **On a separate piece of paper, write a list of five questions you could ask at a job interview. You can use questions on this page or think of your own.**

Unit 11 Test

Before you take the test

Ⓐ Ⓑ Ⓒ Ⓓ | Use the answer sheet for Unit 11 on page 241.

1. Print your name.
2. Print your teacher's name.
3. Write your student identification number, and bubble in the information below the boxes.
4. Write the test date and bubble in the information.
5. Write your class number and bubble in the information.

Listening I [Tracks 78–81]

Listen to the sentence. Which of the following means the same as the sentence you heard: A, B, or C?

1. A. Eric works part-time.

   B. Eric works full-time.

   C. Eric works overtime.

2. A. Experience is required.

   B. I have experience.

   C. Experience is a plus.

3. A. No experience is required.

   B. It has health insurance and paid sick days.

   C. It's not a very good job.

Listening II [Tracks 82–86]

Listen. Questions 4, 5, 6, and 7 are on the audio CD.

Reading

Read. What is the correct answer: A, B, C, or D?

8. Which sentence is correct?

    A. Harry's Hardware Store needs workers.

    B. Harry's Hardware Store doesn't have any job openings now.

    C. Someone at Harry's Hardware Store needs a job.

    D. You should call to apply for a job at Harry's Hardware Store.

9. Which sentence is correct?

    A. The job has no health insurance.

    B. You must speak Spanish for this job.

    C. There is a lot of overtime.

    D. You must go to Harry's if you want to apply for the job.

WANTED
Preschool Teacher

PT, M–F, 15 hrs./week,
$15/hr., no bens.
2 yrs. exp. pref'd
biling. a +
exc. refs. req.
Call 202-555-4567 for more
information or to apply.

10. What is required for this job?

    A. a full-time schedule

    B. benefits

    C. experience

    D. references

11. How can a person apply for the job?

    A. call the phone number

    B. go to the school

    C. get more information

    D. get references

APPLICATION FOR EMPLOYMENT

PART 1 Personal Information

Name: _____

Address: _____ Phone: _____

PART 2 Availability

Desired position: _____ Available starting date: _____

Are you available: _____ full-time _____ part-time _____ overtime
                    _____ days   _____ nights   _____ weekends

PART 3 Education (Begin with present or last school.)

School name and location: _____
_____

From: _____ To: _____ Graduated? _____ Yes _____ No

PART 4 Employment (Begin with present or last job.)

Employer: _____ Address: _____
Phone: _____ Position: _____
From (Month/Year): _____ To (Month/Year): _____
Duties: _____ Supervisor's Name: _____
Reason for Leaving: _____

Employer: _____ Address: _____
Phone: _____ Position: _____
From (Month/Year): _____ To (Month/Year): _____
Duties: _____ Supervisor's Name: _____
Reason for Leaving: _____

PART 5 Skills

Skills (languages, training, equipment or machines) _____

PART 6 References (no family members)

Name	Phone number	Relationship	Years known

12. Where do you write information
    about the job you have now?

    A. Part 2

    B. Part 4

    C. Part 5

    D. Part 6

13. Where do you write about things
    you do well?

    A. Part 5

    B. Part 3

    C. Part 6

    D. Part 1

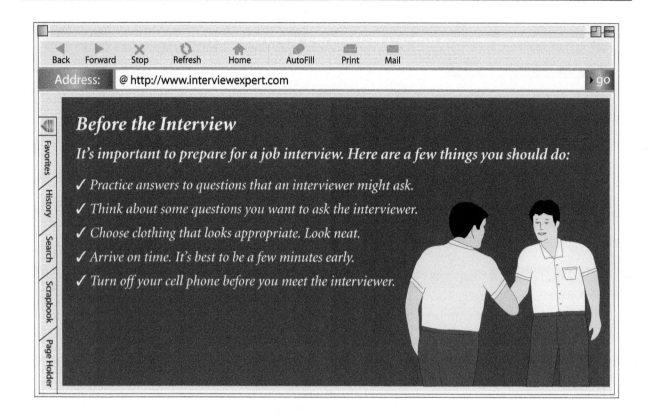

Before the Interview

It's important to prepare for a job interview. Here are a few things you should do:

✓ *Practice answers to questions that an interviewer might ask.*

✓ *Think about some questions you want to ask the interviewer.*

✓ *Choose clothing that looks appropriate. Look neat.*

✓ *Arrive on time. It's best to be a few minutes early.*

✓ *Turn off your cell phone before you meet the interviewer.*

Address: @ http://www.interviewexpert.com

14. What is the purpose of this website?

    A. to explain how to answer interview questions

    B. to explain how to prepare for an interview

    C. to explain how to apply for a job

    D. to explain how to ask questions at an interview

15. What should a person do before an interview?

    A. meet the interviewer

    B. ask the interviewer some questions

    C. practice answers to some interview questions

    D. have a job

Unit 12 At Work

Learn

A   *PAIRS.* **Which words do you know? Match the words with their definitions.**

_c_ 1. manager   a. short period of time during work hours when you stop working

____ 2. employee   b. period of time when someone is at work

____ 3. shift   c. boss, or someone who directs other people at work

____ 4. break   d. day when you don't have to go to work at your job

____ 5. day off   e. worker

B   **Look at part of a work schedule. Complete the sentences. Circle the correct times or words.**

 Builder's Central Hardware Store, Paint Dept.

Employee Work Schedule for Week of 7/14–7/20

	Monday	Tuesday
MANAGERS		
Hung	8:30 – 4:00	8:30 – 4:00
Rina	4:00 – 11:30	4:00 – 11:30
SALESPEOPLE		
Taran	8:30 – 4:00	
Becky	4:00 – 11:30	4:00 – 11:30
Maria		8:30 – 4:00
Felipe	8:30 – 4:00	8:30 – 4:00
Ben	4:00 – 11:30	4:00 – 11:30

Break schedule:
Managers take a ½ hour break 3 ½ hours after shift begins.
Salespeople take a ½ hour break 4 hours after shift begins.

1. The early shift is from (8:30 A.M.–4:00 P.M.)/ 4:00 P.M.–11:30 P.M.
2. Hung and Rina are **managers / salespeople**.
3. Hung, Rina, Taran, and Becky are **employees / managers**.
4. The **early / late** shift starts at 4:00 P.M.
5. **Monday / Tuesday** is Maria's day off.
6. All employees have a half hour **shift / break**.
7. **Managers / Salespeople** take their breaks first.

C   *PAIRS.* **Check your answers.**

Practice

Look at the schedule. Answer the questions.

Electronics Dept.

Work Schedule for Week of 5/19–5/23

	Mon	Tues	Wed	Thurs	Fri
MANAGERS					
Karen	7:00 A.M. 3:00 P.M.	7:00 A.M. 3:00 P.M.	7:00 A.M. 3:00 P.M.	7:00 A.M. 3:00 P.M.	7:00 A.M. 3:00 P.M.
Lan	3:00 P.M. 11:00 P.M.	3:00 P.M. 11:00 P.M.	3:00 P.M. 11:00 P.M.	3:00 P.M. 11:00 P.M.	3:00 P.M. 11:00 P.M.
SALESPEOPLE					
Claudia		7:00 A.M. 3:00 P.M.		7:00 A.M. 3:00 P.M.	
Beth	7:00 A.M. 3:00 P.M.		7:00 A.M. 3:00 P.M.		7:00 A.M. 3:00 P.M.
Rudi	3:00 P.M. 11:00 P.M.		3:00 P.M. 11:00 P.M.		3:00 P.M. 11:00 P.M.
Ivan		3:00 P.M. 11:00 P.M.		3:00 P.M. 11:00 P.M.	
Chris	7:00 A.M. 3:00 P.M.	7:00 A.M. 3:00 P.M.	7:00 A.M. 3:00 P.M.	7:00 A.M. 3:00 P.M.	7:00 A.M. 3:00 P.M.
Amy	3:00 P.M. 11:00 P.M.	3:00 P.M. 11:00 P.M.	3:00 P.M. 11:00 P.M.	3:00 P.M. 11:00 P.M.	3:00 P.M. 11:00 P.M.

Break Schedule:

Managers take a ½ hour break 4 hours after shift begins.

Salespeople take a ½ hour break 3 hours after shift begins.

1. What department do the employees work in? _____

2. How many managers are on the schedule? _____

3. How many managers work during each shift? _____

4. How many employees in total are on the schedule? _____

5. How many employees work the early shift on Thursday? _____

6. Which employees don't work on Wednesday? _____

7. Which salespeople work the early shift on Friday? _____

8. Who takes a break at 11:00 A.M. on Monday? _____

9. How many days does Rudi work this week? _____

10. What time does Lan take his break on Thursday? _____

11. What time does Claudia take her break on Tuesday? _____

Learn

 87   **Listen and read the conversations. Then practice with a partner.**

> **A:** Excuse me, <u>Sima</u>. I don't know <u>who to send this package to</u>.
> **B:** No problem. I can help you.
> **A:** Thanks.

> **A:** Excuse me, <u>Mr. Lee</u>. Could you tell me <u>where to put these boxes</u>?
> **B:** Sure. Just give me a minute.
> **A:** Of course. Thank you.

> **A:** Hi, <u>Ravi</u>. Can you show me <u>how to organize the forms for new employees</u>?
> **B:** Sure. No problem.
> **A:** Great. Thank you.

> **A:** Hey, <u>Gabriela</u>. Can I ask you a favor?
> **B:** Sure. What's up?
> **A:** I'm not sure <u>how to use the new computer program</u>. Can you help me?
> **B:** Yes. I'm a little busy right now, but I'll help you later, OK?
> **A:** Of course. I appreciate it.

Practice

PAIRS. **Practice the conversations again. Use your own names and the information below. Switch roles.**

> You don't know how to make a change to the schedule.
> You don't know what time the new employee meeting starts.
> You don't know how to use the office phone system.
> You don't know who to ask about a problem with your computer.

Make It Yours

CLASS. **In some countries, it's not good to ask a lot of questions at work. What is the tradition in your country? Is it OK to ask questions? Can you ask your boss, or just your co-workers?**

Learn

 Listen and read the conversations. Then practice with a partner.

1. **A:** Sofia, you're usually very careful, but you put these papers in the wrong place. Completed orders should go on the right.
   B: OK. Thanks for explaining it. I'll be sure to put them on the right from now on.

2. **A:** Paco, these files aren't organized correctly.
   B: Oh, I'm sorry about that. Could you show me what's wrong?

3. **A:** Abdul, your work is good, but you talk on the phone too much. You need to limit your personal calls.
   B: I'm sorry. Thanks for telling me. I'll be more careful from now on.

4. **A:** Julia, this is the second time you've been late this month. That's not good.
   B: I'm sorry. I missed the bus. It won't happen again.

Helpful Expressions

✓ Could you show me how to do it again?

✓ Could you explain it to me again?

✓ I'll fix it right away.

✓ I'll remember that.

✓ I'll do better next time.

✓ I'll be more careful from now on.

✓ I'll be sure to . . .

Listen

89 **Listen to the conversations. Complete the sentences. Circle the correct word or phrase.**

1. The boss wants Mateo to **organize his things / say he's sorry**.

2. John will **fix the problem / be more careful** in the future.

3. Alex **apologizes / asks for help**.

4. Sabeer **asked a question / made a mistake**.

5. Ang needs to work **more carefully / more quickly**.

6. Sarita **asks for help / fixes the problem**.

Practice

A **Read the first line of each conversation. Write an appropriate response. Use the responses in Learn and Helpful Expressions on page 197. There is more than one possible answer for each item.**

1. **A:** You filled out this form incorrectly.
   B: _____

2. **A:** You put the new orders in the wrong place. They should go in the box on the left, but you put them in the box on the right.
   B: _____

3. **A:** You're usually a good worker. But today a customer needed help, and there was no one there to help her. That's your responsibility.
   B: _____

4. **A:** Your work is good, but it's never finished on time. You need to work more quickly.
   B: _____

B *PAIRS.* **Compare your answers.**

C *PAIRS. ROLE PLAY.* **Practice the conversations in Exercise A. Switch roles.**

BONUS *PAIRS.* **Tell about a time you were corrected at work. What happened? How did you respond? Would you do anything differently if it happened again?**

Learn

PAIRS. **Look at the pay stub. Which words do you know? Match the words with their definitions.**

Four Brothers' Laundromat

Name	Eva Gomez			Social Security Number	987-65-4321	
Pay period	2 06 09 - 2 20 09			Pay date	2 25 09	
Hourly pay	$10.00			Net pay	$771.08	
Earnings				Deductions		
Pay type	Hours	Amount this period	Amount y-t-d	Type	Amount this period	Amount y-t-d
Regular	80	$800.00	$2,400.00	FICA	$30.40	$121.60
				Fed. Withholding	$107.05	$428.20
Overtime	10	$150.00	$600.00	State Withholding	$24.70	$98.80
				SDI	$16.77	$67.08
Gross pay		$950.00	$3,000.00	Total deductions	$178.92	$715.68

___d___ 1. pay period   a. amount you earned before taxes

_____ 2. pay date   b. amount you earned after taxes

_____ 3. net pay   c. year-to-date; from the beginning of this year until now

_____ 4. earnings   d. time covered by this paycheck

_____ 5. deductions   e. day you are paid

_____ 6. y-t-d   f. amounts taken out of your paycheck for taxes

_____ 7. gross pay   g. money you earn by working

Practice

Look at the pay stub again. Answer the questions.

1. How much money did Eva earn before taxes in this period? _____$950.00_____

2. How much money did Eva earn after taxes in this period? _____

3. How many deductions were taken out of Eva's check? _____

4. How much money was taken out for Federal Withholding in this period? _____

5. How much money has been taken out for SDI so far this year? _____

BONUS   *GROUPS OF 3.* **What is your dream job? What would be the perfect work schedule for you? How much would you get paid?**

Unit 12 Test

 Listening I [Tracks 90–93]

You will hear a conversation. Then you will hear a question about the conversation. What is the correct answer: A, B, or C?

1. What is Anna going to do?

    A. be more careful next time

    B. fix the mistake

    C. explain the problem

2. What is Laura going to do?

    A. ask for help

    B. work more quickly

    C. help the man

3. When will Marie help the woman?

    A. immediately

    B. in a few minutes

    C. tomorrow

 Listening II [Tracks 94–97]

Listen. Questions 4, 5, and 6 are on the audio CD.

Reading

Read. What is the correct answer: A, B, C, or D?

THOMPSON TOOL COMPANY

Employee Weekend Schedule

	Saturday	Sunday
Managers		
Hiro	8:00 A.M.–4:00 P.M.	8:00 A.M.–4:00 P.M.
Julia	4:00 P.M.–12:00 A.M.	4:00 P.M.–12:00 A.M.
Machine Workers		
Soo Chin	4:00 P.M.–12:00 A.M.	4:00 P.M.–12:00 A.M.
Gino	8:00 A.M.–4:00 P.M.	8:00 A.M.–4:00 P.M.
Juanita	8:00 A.M.–4:00 P.M.	4:00 P.M.–12:00 A.M.
Fausto	4:00 P.M.–12:00 A.M.	8:00 A.M.–4:00 P.M.

Break schedule (All breaks are 30 minutes.)

Managers take a break at 12:00 P.M. (for early shift) or 8:00 P.M. (for late shift).

Machine workers take breaks at 12:30 P.M. (for early shift) or 8:30 P.M. (for late shift).

---

7. What time does Fausto take his break on Sunday?

    A. 12:00 P.M.

    B. 12:30 P.M.

    C. 8:00 P.M.

    D. 8:30 P.M.

8. Who works the early shift on Saturday?

    A. Soo Chin, Gino, and Juanita

    B. Hiro, Gino, and Fausto

    C. Julia, Soo Chin, and Fausto

    D. Hiro, Gino, and Juanita

9. How many machine workers work at one time?

    A. two

    B. three

    C. four

    D. one

Elizabeth has a new job in a factory. The factory is big, and people work in two shifts. Elizabeth works the first shift, and she starts work very early in the morning.

Elizabeth is still learning how to do some things at work, and sometimes she has to ask her co-workers or her manager, Angelica, for help. Elizabeth didn't know how to use a new machine, so she asked Angelica. Angelica helped her and showed her how to use the machine.

10. When does Elizabeth work?

A. the early shift

B. the late shift

C. two shifts

D. the second shift

11. What did Angelica do when Elizabeth asked for help?

A. She asked her for a favor.

B. She said to give her a minute.

C. She told the manager.

D. She helped her.

Superb Architects, Inc.

Name	Wes Timberland	**Social Security number**	555-54-3210
Pay period	4/03/09–4/17/09	**Pay date**	4/25/09
Hourly Pay	$22.00	**Net pay**	$1,533.08

EARNINGS				DEDUCTIONS		
Pay type	Hours	Amount this period	Amount y-t-d	Type	Amount this period	Amount y-t-d
Regular	80	$1,760.00	$10,563.00	FICA	$130.40	$782.40
				Fed. Withholding	$307.05	$1,902.30
Overtime	10	$330.00	$990.00	State Withholding	$64.70	$338.20
				SDI	$54.77	$314.62
Gross pay		$2,090.00	$11,553.00	**Total deductions**	$556.92	$3,337.52

12. What is Wes's pay after deductions for this period?

   A. $1,533.08

   B. $556.92

   C. $1,760.00

   D. $3,337.52

13. What is FICA?

   A. a type of earning

   B. a type of deduction

   C. a type of pay

   D. a period of time

14. How much money has Wes made in overtime this year?

   A. $330.00

   B. $990.00

   C. $2,090.00

   D. $11,553.00

15. What is the amount of state withholding for this period?

   A. $556.92

   B. $54.77

   C. $338.20

   D. $64.70

Ivan takes an English class at Central Adult School on Monday, Wednesday, and Friday mornings from 9:00 A.M. to 12:00 P.M. He wants to improve his English for his job. Ivan is an employee at the Chinese Noodle Company. He works the second shift, from 3:00 P.M. to 11:00 P.M., Monday to Saturday. Ivan has a half-hour break during his shift.

16. Where does Ivan work?

    A. Central Adult School

    B. Chinese Noodle Company

    C. second shift

    D. a half-hour break

17. When is Ivan's day off?

    A. Monday

    B. Friday

    C. Saturday

    D. Sunday

Audioscript

Listen page 4

1. Where are you from?
2. Did you graduate from high school?
3. What do you do now?
4. Where did you go to school?
5. When did you come to the United States?
6. Where did you study?

Lesson 3

Learn, Exercise B page 11

I want to improve my English skills to prepare for college courses.

I'm going to take an intermediate ESL course at Vista Adult School.

I'll finish the semester by May 2010.

I want to get accepted to Freemont Community College.

I'm going to complete an application.

I'll send my application by June, 2010.

I want to get my associate degree in early childhood education at FCC.

I'm going to study part-time and take two classes a semester.

I'll get my degree in May 2013.

I want to get a job as a preschool teacher.

I'm going to learn and practice good interview skills.

I'll find a job by December 2013.

Listen page 12

1.

A: Lucy, what are your goals?
B: I want to be a teaching assistant first, and then someday, a teacher.

2.

A: Do you go to school, Javier?
B: Yeah, I study English at night at Valley Adult School.
A: What do you plan to do in the future?
B: I think I'm going to study business at the community college next year.

3.

A: Nina, are you going to look for a job after you finish this English class?
B: No, I'm not going to work. I'm going to take some classes at the community college.

4.

A: I just got my associate degree!
B: Congratulations! What are you going to do next?
A: First I'm going to find a part-time job. Then I'm going to apply to a university. I want to get a bachelor's degree.

Lesson 4

Listen page 15

1.

A: Do you offer any computer classes in the evening?
B: Yes. We have a computer technician class.
A: Great. When does the class meet?

2.

A: I'm interested in a GED class. Do you have evening classes?
B: Yes. Classes are from 7:00 to 9:00 on Mondays, Tuesdays, and Wednesdays.
A: Mondays, Tuesdays, and Wednesdays? OK. Can I register for the class?

3.

A: I'm interested in your automotive technician class. When does the class begin and end?
B: It begins on September 8 and ends on December 4. It's a twelve-week course.

4.

A: Do you have any health classes on weekends?
B: No, but we have a health and wellness class from 6:00 to 8:00 on Mondays.
A: From 6 to 8 on Mondays? OK. Can I register for the class?

UNIT 2 Lesson 1

Listen page 26

Conversation 1

A: Hey, Donna. How's your job going?
B: Ah, it's OK. How's your job?
A: I've been pretty busy, but it's fine.

Conversation 2

A: Hey, Tom. How are the kids?
B: Oh, they're fine thanks. How about yours?

A: Well, Danny is sick, so my wife is home taking care of him.

B: Oh, I'm sorry to hear that.

Conversation 3

A: What a beautiful day!

B: I know. It's really warm for this time of year.

A: I hear that it's going to get cooler over the weekend though.

B: Yeah, I heard that, too.

Conversation 4

A: Have you seen the new Tom Cruise movie?

B: No, I haven't. Have you?

A: Not yet. But I heard that it's really good.

B: Yeah, a friend of mine saw it, and she really liked it.

Conversation 5

A: So, where are you from?

B: El Salvador. How about you?

A: I'm from Korea.

B: How long have you been in the United States?

A: A year. And you?

B: Two years.

UNIT 3 Lesson 1

Learn, **Exercise A** page 38

In the educational system in the United States, children can attend preschool from ages 2 to 5. Preschool is not required.

Children attend elementary school from ages 5 to 11. They start with kindergarten and go to 5th grade. Then, in most places, they go to middle school for grades 6 to 8. After this, they attend a four-year high school for grades 9 to 12.

After students graduate from high school, they have many choices for post-secondary school. They can go to a vocational or technical school, go to a junior or community college, or go to a university or four-year college.

Lesson 2

Learn, **Exercise A** page 41

A: Hi, honey. How was school today?

B: Fine. I got my report card.

A: You did? How did you do?

B: Well, I didn't do so well in English. I got a C+, and Mr. Blair says I need to improve next quarter.

A: Uh-oh. We'll need to talk about that.

B: I know. But, I did really well in math! I got an A.

A: That's wonderful! How did you do in music?

B: I got an A–.

A: That's great!

B: Thanks.

A: And what about your other classes . . . ?

Listen page 43

A: How did you do in history?

B: I did pretty well. I got a B+. How about you?

A: I got a B–.

B: Oh. What did you get in science?

A: A C. What did you get?

B: An A–.

A: Wow, that's good. What did you get in Spanish?

B: A C+. How about you?

A: I got a C+, too.

UNIT 4 Lesson 2

Listen page 51

1.

A: Hello, this is Maria.

B: Hi, this is John. Is Dominic there please?

A: I'm sorry. He's not. Would you like to leave a message?

B: Yeah. Just tell him to call me.

A: OK. No problem.

B: Thanks.

2.

A: Hello, this is Allison.

B: Hi. This is Jeff Thompson. May I please speak to Mr. Hung?

A: I'm sorry. Mr. Hung isn't here. Would you like to leave a message?

B: Yes, please. Please tell him to call me back. He has my number.

A: Could I have your name again?

B: It's Jeff Thompson.

A: OK, Mr. Thompson. I'll tell him.

3.

A: Hello?

B: Hi. Can I talk to Samantha Tomlin, please?

A: Sorry, Samantha's not here.

B: OK. Will you give her a message?

A: Sure.

B: This is Amy Green. Tell her I called. I'll call her again tomorrow.

4.

A: Hello?

B: Hi. This is Sam Frost. Could I talk to Bill Jones?

A: I'm sorry, he's not in. Do you want to leave a message?

B: Yes, please. Tell him to call me back tonight.

A: OK. I'll give him the message.

Practice page 53

1.

A: Hello.

B: Hi, I'm calling from Bright Lighting Company. May I please speak to Mary Sanford?

A: I'm sorry. Mary's not in. Would you like to leave a message?

B: Yes, please. This is Monica Hurley.

A: Could you spell your last name, please?

B: Sure. It's Hurley, H-U-R-L-E-Y.

A: Uh-huh.

B: I'm calling because Mary's order is ready.

A: OK. And what's your number?

B: It's 303-555-1790.

A: OK. You said her order is ready, and your number is 303-555-1790?

B: That's right. Thank you.

A: You're welcome. Good-bye.

2.

A: Hello.

B: Hi. May I please speak to Mr. Ting?

A: I'm sorry. He's not in. Would you like to leave a message?

B: Yes, please. This is Ellen. I'm calling from Dr. Smith's office.

A: Could you spell your name, please?

B: Sure. It's E-L-L-E-N.

A: Uh-huh.

B: I'm calling to confirm his appointment at 3:00 tomorrow. The number is 212-555-4368.

A: OK. You're calling to confirm his appointment tomorrow, and your number is 212-555-4368?

B: That's right. Thank you.

A: You're welcome. Good-bye.

Lesson 4

Learn, Exercise B page 55

1. To hear store hours, press 1.
2. For our location, press 3.
3. For directions to the store, press 5.

Practice page 55

Thank you for calling First Rate Pharmacy, located at the corner of Second Avenue and Grand Street. Please choose from the following menu options.

Doctors, press 9.
For the pharmacy, press 1.
For the photo department, press 2.
For customer service, press 3.
To hear pharmacy hours, press 4.
To hear store hours, press 5.
To hear the options again, press the star key.

Practice page 56

Thank you for calling Fleet City Power and Light.
If you're calling about a problem with your service, press 1.
For billing and payment questions, press 2.
To stop, start, or move service, press 3.
For all other questions, press 4.
To repeat these options, press the star key.
To speak with a representative, press 0.

Practice, Exercise A page 57

Thank you for calling Walcott's Department Store. Please listen carefully to the following options.
To request a catalog, press or say 1 now.
To place an order, press or say 2 now.
To find a store near you, press or say 3 now.
For questions about billing, press or say 4 now.
For customer service, press or say 5 now.

Practice, Exercise B page 57

Thank you for calling the Douglas Museum of Science. The museum is located at 11521 Fairview Avenue. The museum hours are 9:00 A.M. to 6:00 P.M. The museum is open every day of the year except Thanksgiving and Christmas. Tickets and memberships may be bought online 24 hours a day at www.douglassciencemuseum.org or in person at the museum. Admission price for adults is $20. Students with a valid ID and children ages 3–17 pay $15. Children under 3 enter free of charge. For information on current exhibits and show times, please press 1. For information about memberships, please press 2. To speak to a representative during business hours, please press 3. To repeat this information, press 4.

UNIT 5 Lesson 1

Learn, Exercise B page 64

1. Head west.
2. Make a right.
3. Turn left at the light.
4. Go past the stop sign.
5. Turn right onto Grand Avenue.
6. Go straight for two blocks.
7. Go to the intersection of Park and Oak.
8. Spring Avenue is a cross street.

1. Start at Brian's Bookstore. Head west on Highland Street until you get to a stop sign. Make a right onto Taft Avenue. It's the building on your left.
2. Start at the Palace Movie Theater. Head east on Miller Street. At the end of the first block, make a right onto Taft. Go one block, then go east on Robin Street. It's the first building on your right.
3. Start at Anderson Bank. Go north two blocks, and make a left onto Cherry. Continue on Cherry for another block. Cross Adams Avenue. It's the building on your left.
4. Start at the Perla Hotel. Go east on Robin. Make a left at the corner onto Taylor Avenue. Go north two blocks and make a right at the traffic light. Go past the stop sign and continue two more blocks. Cross Ford Ave. The building is on your left.
5. Start at the Lakeview Apartments. Go south on Taft. At the third intersection, go east on Robin. Continue on Robin for one block until you get to a stop sign. Cross that intersection, and it's the building on your left.
6. Start at Garden Market. Go one block east to Ford Avenue and turn left. It's across the street on your right.
7. Start at Cherry Park. Go south on Taylor. At the first intersection, make a left and go two blocks. Cross the next street. It's on your left.

UNIT 6 Lesson 2

Learn, **Exercise B** page 82

1.

A: Can you tell me what train I can take from San Mateo to San Francisco? I need to be in San Francisco by 8:15.

B: The 7:32 gets you to San Francisco at 8:00. It's an express train.

2.

A: Can you tell me what train I can take from San Mateo to Bayshore? I need to be in Bayshore by 8:30.

B: The 7:49 arrives in Bayshore at 8:08.

3.

A: Can you tell me what train I can take from San Mateo to San Francisco? I need to be in San Francisco by 9:00.

B: The 8:07 arrives in San Francisco at 8:48.

4.

A: Can you tell me what train I can take from Hillsdale to San Francisco? I need to be in San Francisco by 10:15.

B. The 9:29 gets you to San Francisco at 10:02.

Learn, **Exercise B** page 84

- Attention passengers. Flight 239 to Chicago is delayed because of a snowstorm in Chicago. The new departure time is 9:40.
- Passengers traveling to Dallas: Flight 302 is now boarding. All passengers on Flight 302 should board now at Gate 65.
- Attention passengers on Flight 811 to Denver: This flight is delayed because of heavy rain. The new departure time is 8:10.
- Attention: North Star Flight 422 to Miami is canceled because of mechanical problems. All passengers with tickets for Flight 422, please see a gate attendant.
- Passengers on Flight 102 to San Antonio: Your flight has been delayed because of mechanical problems. The new departure time is 9:15.
- We are now boarding Flight 262 to San Francisco at Gate 85. Passengers on Flight 262 please begin boarding at Gate 85.

Practice, **Exercise C** page 85

Welcome aboard Flight 811 with service to Los Angeles. Our estimated flight time is two hours and twenty minutes. Our estimated arrival time in Los Angeles is 1:00 local time.

Listen page 85

1. Attention passengers: The 8:45 bus to Boston is delayed and is now scheduled to leave at 9:15.
2. Attention: Flight 202 to Houston is delayed due to bad weather.
3. The 10:22 train from Rockville to Washington, D.C., is canceled due to mechanical problems.
4. Attention: All bus service to Chicago is canceled due to bad weather.
5. There will be a fifteen-minute delay on all trains leaving from Baltimore due to mechanical problems.

Lesson 3,

Learn, **Exercise A** page 86

rearview mirror
windshield
windshield wiper
headlight
hood
tire
hubcap
sideview mirror

brake light
trunk
bumper
license plate
exhaust pipe
turn signal
taillight

Learn, **Exercise A** page 88

dashboard
steering wheel
gas pedal
brake pedal
gear shift
emergency brake

Learn, **Exercise B** page 88

seat belt
lock
back seat
child safety seat
front seat

Lesson 4

Learn, **Exercise B** page 90

1. get gas
2. check the tire pressure
3. check the oil
4. add coolant and other fluids

UNIT 7 Lesson 1

Listen page 101

1. **Conversation 1**
A: I need to go to an ATM.
B: Me, too. I have to take out some money.

2. **Conversation 2**
A: How often do you get paid?
B: Every Friday. The company puts my paycheck directly into my checking account.

3. **Conversation 3**
A: I'm going to open a new bank account.
B: Oh yeah?
A: Yeah. I want an account that pays me interest.

4. **Conversation 4**
A: Do you have a checking account?
B: Yes, I do. And I don't have to pay anything for it. It's free.

Lesson 2

Learn page 106

1. The statement date is the day the credit card company sent you the statement.
2. The payment due date is the last day you can pay this bill.
3. The credit limit is the total amount of money you can spend with this card.
4. The credit available is the total amount you can spend with this card minus the amount you already owe.
5. The new balance is the amount of money you owe the credit card company this month.
6. The minimum payment due is the smallest amount of money you can pay the credit card company.
7. This is a list of the transactions made with the card this month.
8. The previous balance is the amount you owed last month.
9. New purchases show the total amount you spent with the card this month.
10. A cash advance is money you borrowed from your credit card company.
11. Interest is extra money you have to pay because you didn't pay the full amount you owed last month.
12. Payments are money you paid the credit card company last month.
13. The payment coupon is the part of the bill you send to the credit card company with your payment.

Lesson 3

Listen page 109

1. A: Can you tell me about the house for rent?
   B: Sure. It has two bedrooms and one bathroom, and it has a large yard.
2. A: How much is the rent?
   B: It's $900 a month, plus utilities.
3. A: Is the apartment near transportation?
   B: Yes, it's one block from a bus stop.
4. A: Is there a place to park my car?
   B: Yes, there's a garage.
5. A: Does the apartment have a washer and dryer?
   B: Yes, it does.

UNIT 8 Lesson 1

Learn, **Exercise B** page 121

1. simmer
2. chop
3. drain

4. mix / stir

5. slice

6. boil

7. melt

8. season

Listen page 124

1. Cook the chicken in 1 tablespoon of oil until it's no longer pink, about 8 minutes. Set it aside.

2. Add the pasta to eight cups of boiling water. Cook until tender, about 9 minutes.

3. Drain the pasta.

4. Mix the seasoning with one-third cup of hot milk and 3 tablespoons of melted butter.

5. Add the mixture to the pasta.

6. Add the chicken and stir.

Lesson 2

Listen page 129

1.

A: How much are these shoes?

B: Well, the regular price is $35, but they're on sale now for $25.

2.

A: What's the discount on this shirt?

B: It's 40% off.

3.

A: Is this jacket on sale?

B: Yes, it is. It's just $20.

4.

A: When's the sale?

B: Tomorrow only. And you can save an additional 10% if you shop before 11:00 A.M.

5.

A: Are women's pants on sale?

B: Yes, all women's pants are $10 off the regular price.

UNIT 9 Lesson 1

Listen page 144

1.

A: Hey, Tony! What are you doing for Labor Day?

B: I'm having a picnic with my family. I'm going to relax!

2.

A: What are your plans for Independence Day?

B: Well, at night we're going to watch fireworks.

3.

A: Hey—we don't have classes next Monday.

B: I know. It's Martin Luther King Day. My friends and I are going to do some work in our community since we don't have class.

Learn, **Exercise A** page 145

The U.S. Constitution is the highest law of our country. It explains that there are three branches, or parts, which make up the federal government. The three parts are the legislative branch, the executive branch, and the judicial branch.

The legislative branch includes the members of Congress. Congress has two parts: The House of Representatives and the Senate. There are 435 representatives in the House of Representatives and 100 senators in the Senate.

The president is the head of the executive branch. The vice president helps the president. The president chooses cabinet members to direct different government departments.

The judicial branch includes the Supreme Court. The Supreme Court is the highest court in the country. There are nine judges on the Supreme Court.

UNIT 10 Lesson 4

Listen page 163

1. So, what's the problem?

2. What seems to be the matter?

3. How long has this been going on?

4. How often does this happen?

UNIT 11 Lesson 2

Listen page 180

1. Frank works 25 hours a week.

2. Rita's Restaurant is hiring part-time workers. Apply in person at the restaurant.

3. People with experience are preferred for this job.

4. The job pays $12 an hour.

5. Marta is going to apply for a job at The Super Market.

6. Call Don to apply for the job.

UNIT 12 Lesson 2

Listen page 198

1.

A: Mateo, your workspace is very disorganized. You need to organize your things.

B: I'm sorry. I'll do it today.

2.

A: John, you counted the boxes wrong. There are 35 boxes here, not 34.

B: I'm sorry. I'll be more careful next time.

3.

A: Alex, you were late for work again today.

B: I'm sorry. There was a lot of traffic. It won't happen again.

4.

A: Sabeer, you didn't do this correctly.

B: I'm sorry. I'll fix it right away.

5.

A: Ang, you work too quickly, and you sometimes make mistakes.

B: I'm sorry. I'll work more carefully from now on.

6.

A: Sarita, you made a mistake with this form.

B: I'm sorry. Could you show me what I did wrong?

Life Skills and Test Prep 3
Unit 1 Test Answer Sheet

① _____

    Last Name   First Name   Middle

② _____

    Teacher's Name

TEST

1 Ⓐ Ⓑ Ⓒ Ⓓ
2 Ⓐ Ⓑ Ⓒ Ⓓ
3 Ⓐ Ⓑ Ⓒ Ⓓ
4 Ⓐ Ⓑ Ⓒ Ⓓ
5 Ⓐ Ⓑ Ⓒ Ⓓ
6 Ⓐ Ⓑ Ⓒ Ⓓ
7 Ⓐ Ⓑ Ⓒ Ⓓ
8 Ⓐ Ⓑ Ⓒ Ⓓ
9 Ⓐ Ⓑ Ⓒ Ⓓ
10 Ⓐ Ⓑ Ⓒ Ⓓ
11 Ⓐ Ⓑ Ⓒ Ⓓ
12 Ⓐ Ⓑ Ⓒ Ⓓ
13 Ⓐ Ⓑ Ⓒ Ⓓ
14 Ⓐ Ⓑ Ⓒ Ⓓ
15 Ⓐ Ⓑ Ⓒ Ⓓ
16 Ⓐ Ⓑ Ⓒ Ⓓ
17 Ⓐ Ⓑ Ⓒ Ⓓ
18 Ⓐ Ⓑ Ⓒ Ⓓ
19 Ⓐ Ⓑ Ⓒ Ⓓ
20 Ⓐ Ⓑ Ⓒ Ⓓ

Directions for marking answers

- Use a No. 2 pencil. Do NOT use ink.
- Make dark marks and bubble in your answers completely.
- If you change an answer, erase your first mark completely.

Right
Ⓐ Ⓑ Ⓒ Ⓓ

Wrong
Ⓐ Ⓧ Ⓒ Ⓓ
Ⓐ Ⓑ Ⓒ Ⓓ

③ **STUDENT IDENTIFICATION**

0 0 0 0 0 0 0 0 0
1 1 1 1 1 1 1 1 1
2 2 2 2 2 2 2 2 2
3 3 3 3 3 3 3 3 3
4 4 4 4 4 4 4 4 4
5 5 5 5 5 5 5 5 5
6 6 6 6 6 6 6 6 6
7 7 7 7 7 7 7 7 7
8 8 8 8 8 8 8 8 8
9 9 9 9 9 9 9 9 9

Is this your Social Security number?
Yes ☐   No ☐

④ **TEST DATE**

MM	D	D	Y	Y
Jan	0	0	200	0
Feb	1	1	200	1
Mar	2	2	200	2
Apr	3	3	200	3
May		4	200	4
Jun		5	200	5
Jul		6	200	6
Aug		7	200	7
Sep		8	200	8
Oct		9	200	9
Nov				
Dec				

⑤ **CLASS NUMBER**

0 0 0 0 0 0 0 0
1 1 1 1 1 1 1 1
2 2 2 2 2 2 2 2
3 3 3 3 3 3 3 3
4 4 4 4 4 4 4 4
5 5 5 5 5 5 5 5
6 6 6 6 6 6 6 6
7 7 7 7 7 7 7 7
8 8 8 8 8 8 8 8
9 9 9 9 9 9 9 9

⑥ **RAW SCORE**

0 0
1 1
2 2
3 3
4 4
5 5
6 6
7 7
8 8
9 9

Life Skills and Test Prep 3
Unit 1 Test Answer Sheet

① _____
   Last Name   First Name   Middle

② _____
   Teacher's Name

TEST

1 Ⓐ Ⓑ Ⓒ Ⓓ
2 Ⓐ Ⓑ Ⓒ Ⓓ
3 Ⓐ Ⓑ Ⓒ Ⓓ
4 Ⓐ Ⓑ Ⓒ Ⓓ
5 Ⓐ Ⓑ Ⓒ Ⓓ
6 Ⓐ Ⓑ Ⓒ Ⓓ
7 Ⓐ Ⓑ Ⓒ Ⓓ
8 Ⓐ Ⓑ Ⓒ Ⓓ
9 Ⓐ Ⓑ Ⓒ Ⓓ
10 Ⓐ Ⓑ Ⓒ Ⓓ
11 Ⓐ Ⓑ Ⓒ Ⓓ
12 Ⓐ Ⓑ Ⓒ Ⓓ
13 Ⓐ Ⓑ Ⓒ Ⓓ
14 Ⓐ Ⓑ Ⓒ Ⓓ
15 Ⓐ Ⓑ Ⓒ Ⓓ
16 Ⓐ Ⓑ Ⓒ Ⓓ
17 Ⓐ Ⓑ Ⓒ Ⓓ
18 Ⓐ Ⓑ Ⓒ Ⓓ
19 Ⓐ Ⓑ Ⓒ Ⓓ
20 Ⓐ Ⓑ Ⓒ Ⓓ

Directions for marking answers

- Use a No. 2 pencil. Do NOT use ink.
- Make dark marks and bubble in your answers completely.
- If you change an answer, erase your first mark completely.

Right
Ⓐ ⬤Ⓑ Ⓒ Ⓓ

Wrong
Ⓐ ⊗ Ⓒ Ⓓ
Ⓐ Ⓑ Ⓒ Ⓓ

③ STUDENT IDENTIFICATION

0 0 0	0 0	0 0 0 0
1 1 1	1 1	1 1 1 1
2 2 2	2 2	2 2 2 2
3 3 3	3 3	3 3 3 3
4 4 4	4 4	4 4 4 4
5 5 5	5 5	5 5 5 5
6 6 6	6 6	6 6 6 6
7 7 7	7 7	7 7 7 7
8 8 8	8 8	8 8 8 8
9 9 9	9 9	9 9 9 9

Is this your Social Security number?
Yes ◯   No ◯

④ TEST DATE

MM	D	D	Y	Y
Jan ◯	0	0	200	0
Feb ◯	1	1	200	1
Mar ◯	2	2	200	2
Apr ◯	3	3	200	3
May ◯		4	200	4
Jun ◯		5	200	5
Jul ◯		6	200	6
Aug ◯		7	200	7
Sep ◯		8	200	8
Oct ◯		9	200	9
Nov ◯				
Dec ◯				

⑤ CLASS NUMBER

| 0 0 0 0 0 0 0 0 |
| 1 1 1 1 1 1 1 1 |
| 2 2 2 2 2 2 2 2 |
| 3 3 3 3 3 3 3 3 |
| 4 4 4 4 4 4 4 4 |
| 5 5 5 5 5 5 5 5 |
| 6 6 6 6 6 6 6 6 |
| 7 7 7 7 7 7 7 7 |
| 8 8 8 8 8 8 8 8 |
| 9 9 9 9 9 9 9 9 |

⑥ RAW SCORE

| 0 0 |
| 1 1 |
| 2 2 |
| 3 3 |
| 4 4 |
| 5 5 |
| 6 6 |
| 7 7 |
| 8 8 |
| 9 9 |

Life Skills and Test Prep 3
Unit 2 Test Answer Sheet

① _____

Last Name   First Name   Middle

② _____

Teacher's Name

TEST

1 Ⓐ Ⓑ Ⓒ Ⓓ
2 Ⓐ Ⓑ Ⓒ Ⓓ
3 Ⓐ Ⓑ Ⓒ Ⓓ
4 Ⓐ Ⓑ Ⓒ Ⓓ
5 Ⓐ Ⓑ Ⓒ Ⓓ
6 Ⓐ Ⓑ Ⓒ Ⓓ
7 Ⓐ Ⓑ Ⓒ Ⓓ
8 Ⓐ Ⓑ Ⓒ Ⓓ
9 Ⓐ Ⓑ Ⓒ Ⓓ
10 Ⓐ Ⓑ Ⓒ Ⓓ
11 Ⓐ Ⓑ Ⓒ Ⓓ
12 Ⓐ Ⓑ Ⓒ Ⓓ
13 Ⓐ Ⓑ Ⓒ Ⓓ
14 Ⓐ Ⓑ Ⓒ Ⓓ
15 Ⓐ Ⓑ Ⓒ Ⓓ
16 Ⓐ Ⓑ Ⓒ Ⓓ
17 Ⓐ Ⓑ Ⓒ Ⓓ
18 Ⓐ Ⓑ Ⓒ Ⓓ
19 Ⓐ Ⓑ Ⓒ Ⓓ
20 Ⓐ Ⓑ Ⓒ Ⓓ

Directions for marking answers

- Use a No. 2 pencil. Do NOT use ink.
- Make dark marks and bubble in your answers completely.
- If you change an answer, erase your first mark completely.

Right
Ⓐ ⬤Ⓑ Ⓒ Ⓓ

Wrong
Ⓐ ⓧ Ⓒ Ⓓ
Ⓐ Ⓑ Ⓒ Ⓓ

③ **STUDENT IDENTIFICATION**

0 0 0 0 0 0 0 0
1 1 1 1 1 1 1 1
2 2 2 2 2 2 2 2
3 3 3 3 3 3 3 3
4 4 4 4 4 4 4 4
5 5 5 5 5 5 5 5
6 6 6 6 6 6 6 6
7 7 7 7 7 7 7 7
8 8 8 8 8 8 8 8
9 9 9 9 9 9 9 9

Is this your Social Security number?
Yes ⬭   No ⬭

④ **TEST DATE**

MM	D	D	Y	Y
Jan	0	0	200	0
Feb	1	1	200	1
Mar	2	2	200	2
Apr	3	3	200	3
May		4	200	4
Jun		5	200	5
Jul		6	200	6
Aug		7	200	7
Sep		8	200	8
Oct		9	200	9
Nov				
Dec				

⑤ **CLASS NUMBER**

0 0 0 0 0 0 0 0
1 1 1 1 1 1 1 1
2 2 2 2 2 2 2 2
3 3 3 3 3 3 3 3
4 4 4 4 4 4 4 4
5 5 5 5 5 5 5 5
6 6 6 6 6 6 6 6
7 7 7 7 7 7 7 7
8 8 8 8 8 8 8 8
9 9 9 9 9 9 9 9

⑥ **RAW SCORE**

0 0
1 1
2 2
3 3
4 4
5 5
6 6
7 7
8 8
9 9

Life Skills and Test Prep 3
Unit 2 Test Answer Sheet

① _____

Last Name   First Name   Middle

② _____

Teacher's Name

TEST

1. Ⓐ Ⓑ Ⓒ Ⓓ
2. Ⓐ Ⓑ Ⓒ Ⓓ
3. Ⓐ Ⓑ Ⓒ Ⓓ
4. Ⓐ Ⓑ Ⓒ Ⓓ
5. Ⓐ Ⓑ Ⓒ Ⓓ
6. Ⓐ Ⓑ Ⓒ Ⓓ
7. Ⓐ Ⓑ Ⓒ Ⓓ
8. Ⓐ Ⓑ Ⓒ Ⓓ
9. Ⓐ Ⓑ Ⓒ Ⓓ
10. Ⓐ Ⓑ Ⓒ Ⓓ
11. Ⓐ Ⓑ Ⓒ Ⓓ
12. Ⓐ Ⓑ Ⓒ Ⓓ
13. Ⓐ Ⓑ Ⓒ Ⓓ
14. Ⓐ Ⓑ Ⓒ Ⓓ
15. Ⓐ Ⓑ Ⓒ Ⓓ
16. Ⓐ Ⓑ Ⓒ Ⓓ
17. Ⓐ Ⓑ Ⓒ Ⓓ
18. Ⓐ Ⓑ Ⓒ Ⓓ
19. Ⓐ Ⓑ Ⓒ Ⓓ
20. Ⓐ Ⓑ Ⓒ Ⓓ

Directions for marking answers

- Use a No. 2 pencil. Do NOT use ink.
- Make dark marks and bubble in your answers completely.
- If you change an answer, erase your first mark completely.

Right
Ⓐ ⬤B Ⓒ Ⓓ

Wrong
Ⓐ ⓧ Ⓒ Ⓓ
Ⓐ Ⓑ Ⓒ Ⓓ

③ **STUDENT IDENTIFICATION**

(grid of bubbles 0–9)

Is this your Social Security number?
Yes ◯ No ◯

④ **TEST DATE**

MM	D	D	Y	Y
Jan	0	0	200	0
Feb	1	1	200	1
Mar	2	2	200	2
Apr	3	3	200	3
May		4	200	4
Jun		5	200	5
Jul		6	200	6
Aug		7	200	7
Sep		8	200	8
Oct		9	200	9
Nov				
Dec				

⑤ **CLASS NUMBER**

(grid of bubbles 0–9)

⑥ **RAW SCORE**

(grid of bubbles 0–9)

Life Skills and Test Prep 3
Unit 3 Test Answer Sheet

① _____

Last Name   First Name   Middle

② _____

Teacher's Name

TEST

1 Ⓐ Ⓑ Ⓒ Ⓓ
2 Ⓐ Ⓑ Ⓒ Ⓓ
3 Ⓐ Ⓑ Ⓒ Ⓓ
4 Ⓐ Ⓑ Ⓒ Ⓓ
5 Ⓐ Ⓑ Ⓒ Ⓓ
6 Ⓐ Ⓑ Ⓒ Ⓓ
7 Ⓐ Ⓑ Ⓒ Ⓓ
8 Ⓐ Ⓑ Ⓒ Ⓓ
9 Ⓐ Ⓑ Ⓒ Ⓓ
10 Ⓐ Ⓑ Ⓒ Ⓓ
11 Ⓐ Ⓑ Ⓒ Ⓓ
12 Ⓐ Ⓑ Ⓒ Ⓓ
13 Ⓐ Ⓑ Ⓒ Ⓓ
14 Ⓐ Ⓑ Ⓒ Ⓓ
15 Ⓐ Ⓑ Ⓒ Ⓓ
16 Ⓐ Ⓑ Ⓒ Ⓓ
17 Ⓐ Ⓑ Ⓒ Ⓓ
18 Ⓐ Ⓑ Ⓒ Ⓓ
19 Ⓐ Ⓑ Ⓒ Ⓓ
20 Ⓐ Ⓑ Ⓒ Ⓓ

Directions for marking answers

- Use a No. 2 pencil. Do NOT use ink.
- Make dark marks and bubble in your answers completely.
- If you change an answer, erase your first mark completely.

Right
Ⓐ ⬤Ⓑ Ⓒ Ⓓ

Wrong
Ⓐ ⊗ Ⓒ Ⓓ
Ⓐ Ⓑ Ⓒ Ⓓ

③ STUDENT IDENTIFICATION

| 0 0 0 0 0 0 0 0 0 |
| 1 1 1 1 1 1 1 1 1 |
| 2 2 2 2 2 2 2 2 2 |
| 3 3 3 3 3 3 3 3 3 |
| 4 4 4 4 4 4 4 4 4 |
| 5 5 5 5 5 5 5 5 5 |
| 6 6 6 6 6 6 6 6 6 |
| 7 7 7 7 7 7 7 7 7 |
| 8 8 8 8 8 8 8 8 8 |
| 9 9 9 9 9 9 9 9 9 |

Is this your Social Security number?
Yes ◯   No ◯

④ TEST DATE

MM	D	D	Y	Y
Jan	0	0	200	0
Feb	1	1	200	1
Mar	2	2	200	2
Apr	3	3	200	3
May		4	200	4
Jun		5	200	5
Jul		6	200	6
Aug		7	200	7
Sep		8	200	8
Oct		9	200	9
Nov				
Dec				

⑤ CLASS NUMBER

| 0 0 0 0 0 0 0 0 |
| 1 1 1 1 1 1 1 1 |
| 2 2 2 2 2 2 2 2 |
| 3 3 3 3 3 3 3 3 |
| 4 4 4 4 4 4 4 4 |
| 5 5 5 5 5 5 5 5 |
| 6 6 6 6 6 6 6 6 |
| 7 7 7 7 7 7 7 7 |
| 8 8 8 8 8 8 8 8 |
| 9 9 9 9 9 9 9 9 |

⑥ RAW SCORE

| 0 0 |
| 1 1 |
| 2 2 |
| 3 3 |
| 4 4 |
| 5 5 |
| 6 6 |
| 7 7 |
| 8 8 |
| 9 9 |

Life Skills and Test Prep 3
Unit 3 Test Answer Sheet

① _____

    Last Name   First Name   Middle

② _____

    Teacher's Name

TEST

1 Ⓐ Ⓑ Ⓒ Ⓓ
2 Ⓐ Ⓑ Ⓒ Ⓓ
3 Ⓐ Ⓑ Ⓒ Ⓓ
4 Ⓐ Ⓑ Ⓒ Ⓓ
5 Ⓐ Ⓑ Ⓒ Ⓓ
6 Ⓐ Ⓑ Ⓒ Ⓓ
7 Ⓐ Ⓑ Ⓒ Ⓓ
8 Ⓐ Ⓑ Ⓒ Ⓓ
9 Ⓐ Ⓑ Ⓒ Ⓓ
10 Ⓐ Ⓑ Ⓒ Ⓓ
11 Ⓐ Ⓑ Ⓒ Ⓓ
12 Ⓐ Ⓑ Ⓒ Ⓓ
13 Ⓐ Ⓑ Ⓒ Ⓓ
14 Ⓐ Ⓑ Ⓒ Ⓓ
15 Ⓐ Ⓑ Ⓒ Ⓓ
16 Ⓐ Ⓑ Ⓒ Ⓓ
17 Ⓐ Ⓑ Ⓒ Ⓓ
18 Ⓐ Ⓑ Ⓒ Ⓓ
19 Ⓐ Ⓑ Ⓒ Ⓓ
20 Ⓐ Ⓑ Ⓒ Ⓓ

Directions for marking answers

- Use a No. 2 pencil. Do NOT use ink.
- Make dark marks and bubble in your answers completely.
- If you change an answer, erase your first mark completely.

Right
Ⓐ Ⓑ Ⓒ Ⓓ

Wrong
Ⓐ Ⓧ Ⓒ Ⓓ
Ⓐ Ⓑ Ⓒ Ⓓ

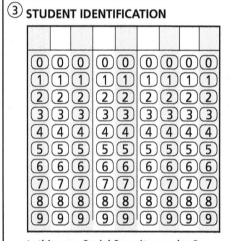

③ **STUDENT IDENTIFICATION**

Is this your Social Security number?
Yes ◯ No ◯

④ **TEST DATE**

MM		D	D	Y	Y
Jan ◯		0	0	200	0
Feb ◯		1	1	200	1
Mar ◯		2	2	200	2
Apr ◯		3	3	200	3
May ◯			4	200	4
Jun ◯			5	200	5
Jul ◯			6	200	6
Aug ◯			7	200	7
Sep ◯			8	200	8
Oct ◯			9	200	9
Nov ◯					
Dec ◯					

⑤ **CLASS NUMBER**

⑥ **RAW SCORE**

Life Skills and Test Prep 3
Unit 4 Test Answer Sheet

① _____

    Last Name   First Name   Middle

② _____

    Teacher's Name

TEST

1 (A) (B) (C) (D)
2 (A) (B) (C) (D)
3 (A) (B) (C) (D)
4 (A) (B) (C) (D)
5 (A) (B) (C) (D)
6 (A) (B) (C) (D)
7 (A) (B) (C) (D)
8 (A) (B) (C) (D)
9 (A) (B) (C) (D)
10 (A) (B) (C) (D)
11 (A) (B) (C) (D)
12 (A) (B) (C) (D)
13 (A) (B) (C) (D)
14 (A) (B) (C) (D)
15 (A) (B) (C) (D)
16 (A) (B) (C) (D)
17 (A) (B) (C) (D)
18 (A) (B) (C) (D)
19 (A) (B) (C) (D)
20 (A) (B) (C) (D)

Directions for marking answers

- Use a No. 2 pencil. Do NOT use ink.
- Make dark marks and bubble in your answers completely.
- If you change an answer, erase your first mark completely.

Right
(A) (B) (C) (D)

Wrong
(A) (X) (C) (D)
(A) (B) (C) (D)

③ STUDENT IDENTIFICATION

0	0	0	0	0	0	0	0	0
1	1	1	1	1	1	1	1	1
2	2	2	2	2	2	2	2	2
3	3	3	3	3	3	3	3	3
4	4	4	4	4	4	4	4	4
5	5	5	5	5	5	5	5	5
6	6	6	6	6	6	6	6	6
7	7	7	7	7	7	7	7	7
8	8	8	8	8	8	8	8	8
9	9	9	9	9	9	9	9	9

Is this your Social Security number?
Yes ☐ No ☐

④ TEST DATE

MM	D	D	Y	Y
Jan ☐	0	0	200	0
Feb ☐	1	1	200	1
Mar ☐	2	2	200	2
Apr ☐	3	3	200	3
May ☐		4	200	4
Jun ☐		5	200	5
Jul ☐		6	200	6
Aug ☐		7	200	7
Sep ☐		8	200	8
Oct ☐		9	200	9
Nov ☐				
Dec ☐				

⑤ CLASS NUMBER

0	0	0	0	0	0	0	0
1	1	1	1	1	1	1	1
2	2	2	2	2	2	2	2
3	3	3	3	3	3	3	3
4	4	4	4	4	4	4	4
5	5	5	5	5	5	5	5
6	6	6	6	6	6	6	6
7	7	7	7	7	7	7	7
8	8	8	8	8	8	8	8
9	9	9	9	9	9	9	9

⑥ RAW SCORE

0	0
1	1
2	2
3	3
4	4
5	5
6	6
7	7
8	8
9	9

Life Skills and Test Prep 3
Unit 4 Test Answer Sheet

① _____

    Last Name   First Name   Middle

② _____

    Teacher's Name

TEST

1 Ⓐ Ⓑ Ⓒ Ⓓ
2 Ⓐ Ⓑ Ⓒ Ⓓ
3 Ⓐ Ⓑ Ⓒ Ⓓ
4 Ⓐ Ⓑ Ⓒ Ⓓ
5 Ⓐ Ⓑ Ⓒ Ⓓ
6 Ⓐ Ⓑ Ⓒ Ⓓ
7 Ⓐ Ⓑ Ⓒ Ⓓ
8 Ⓐ Ⓑ Ⓒ Ⓓ
9 Ⓐ Ⓑ Ⓒ Ⓓ
10 Ⓐ Ⓑ Ⓒ Ⓓ
11 Ⓐ Ⓑ Ⓒ Ⓓ
12 Ⓐ Ⓑ Ⓒ Ⓓ
13 Ⓐ Ⓑ Ⓒ Ⓓ
14 Ⓐ Ⓑ Ⓒ Ⓓ
15 Ⓐ Ⓑ Ⓒ Ⓓ
16 Ⓐ Ⓑ Ⓒ Ⓓ
17 Ⓐ Ⓑ Ⓒ Ⓓ
18 Ⓐ Ⓑ Ⓒ Ⓓ
19 Ⓐ Ⓑ Ⓒ Ⓓ
20 Ⓐ Ⓑ Ⓒ Ⓓ

Directions for marking answers

- Use a No. 2 pencil. Do NOT use ink.
- Make dark marks and bubble in your answers completely.
- If you change an answer, erase your first mark completely.

Right
Ⓐ ⬛ Ⓒ Ⓓ

Wrong
Ⓐ ⓧ Ⓒ Ⓓ
Ⓐ Ⓑ Ⓒ Ⓓ

③ **STUDENT IDENTIFICATION**

(grid of bubbles 0–9 across nine columns)

Is this your Social Security number?
Yes ◯   No ◯

④ **TEST DATE**

MM	D	D	Y	Y
Jan	0	0	200	0
Feb	1	1	200	1
Mar	2	2	200	2
Apr	3	3	200	3
May		4	200	4
Jun		5	200	5
Jul		6	200	6
Aug		7	200	7
Sep		8	200	8
Oct		9	200	9
Nov				
Dec				

⑤ **CLASS NUMBER**

(grid of bubbles 0–9 across eight columns)

⑥ **RAW SCORE**

(grid of bubbles 0–9 across two columns)

Life Skills and Test Prep 3
Unit 5 Test Answer Sheet

① _____
　　 Last Name　　　　　　First Name　　　　Middle

② _____
　　 Teacher's Name

TEST

1　Ⓐ Ⓑ Ⓒ Ⓓ
2　Ⓐ Ⓑ Ⓒ Ⓓ
3　Ⓐ Ⓑ Ⓒ Ⓓ
4　Ⓐ Ⓑ Ⓒ Ⓓ
5　Ⓐ Ⓑ Ⓒ Ⓓ
6　Ⓐ Ⓑ Ⓒ Ⓓ
7　Ⓐ Ⓑ Ⓒ Ⓓ
8　Ⓐ Ⓑ Ⓒ Ⓓ
9　Ⓐ Ⓑ Ⓒ Ⓓ
10　Ⓐ Ⓑ Ⓒ Ⓓ
11　Ⓐ Ⓑ Ⓒ Ⓓ
12　Ⓐ Ⓑ Ⓒ Ⓓ
13　Ⓐ Ⓑ Ⓒ Ⓓ
14　Ⓐ Ⓑ Ⓒ Ⓓ
15　Ⓐ Ⓑ Ⓒ Ⓓ
16　Ⓐ Ⓑ Ⓒ Ⓓ
17　Ⓐ Ⓑ Ⓒ Ⓓ
18　Ⓐ Ⓑ Ⓒ Ⓓ
19　Ⓐ Ⓑ Ⓒ Ⓓ
20　Ⓐ Ⓑ Ⓒ Ⓓ

Directions for marking answers

- Use a No. 2 pencil. Do NOT use ink.
- Make dark marks and bubble in your answers completely.
- If you change an answer, erase your first mark completely.

Right
Ⓐ Ⓑ Ⓒ Ⓓ
Wrong
Ⓐ Ⓧ Ⓒ Ⓓ
Ⓐ Ⓑ Ⓒ Ⓓ

③ **STUDENT IDENTIFICATION**

Is this your Social Security number?
Yes ◯　No ◯

④ **TEST DATE**

MM	D	D	Y	Y
Jan	0	0	200	0
Feb	1	1	200	1
Mar	2	2	200	2
Apr	3	3	200	3
May		4	200	4
Jun		5	200	5
Jul		6	200	6
Aug		7	200	7
Sep		8	200	8
Oct		9	200	9
Nov				
Dec				

⑤ **CLASS NUMBER**

⑥ **RAW SCORE**

Life Skills and Test Prep 3
Unit 5 Test Answer Sheet

① _____

Last Name   First Name   Middle

② _____

Teacher's Name

TEST

1 Ⓐ Ⓑ Ⓒ Ⓓ
2 Ⓐ Ⓑ Ⓒ Ⓓ
3 Ⓐ Ⓑ Ⓒ Ⓓ
4 Ⓐ Ⓑ Ⓒ Ⓓ
5 Ⓐ Ⓑ Ⓒ Ⓓ
6 Ⓐ Ⓑ Ⓒ Ⓓ
7 Ⓐ Ⓑ Ⓒ Ⓓ
8 Ⓐ Ⓑ Ⓒ Ⓓ
9 Ⓐ Ⓑ Ⓒ Ⓓ
10 Ⓐ Ⓑ Ⓒ Ⓓ
11 Ⓐ Ⓑ Ⓒ Ⓓ
12 Ⓐ Ⓑ Ⓒ Ⓓ
13 Ⓐ Ⓑ Ⓒ Ⓓ
14 Ⓐ Ⓑ Ⓒ Ⓓ
15 Ⓐ Ⓑ Ⓒ Ⓓ
16 Ⓐ Ⓑ Ⓒ Ⓓ
17 Ⓐ Ⓑ Ⓒ Ⓓ
18 Ⓐ Ⓑ Ⓒ Ⓓ
19 Ⓐ Ⓑ Ⓒ Ⓓ
20 Ⓐ Ⓑ Ⓒ Ⓓ

Directions for marking answers

- Use a No. 2 pencil. DO NOT use ink.
- Make dark marks and bubble in your answers completely.
- If you change an answer, erase your first mark completely.

Right
Ⓐ Ⓑ Ⓒ Ⓓ

Wrong
Ⓐ Ⓧ Ⓒ Ⓓ
Ⓐ Ⓑ Ⓒ Ⓓ

③ STUDENT IDENTIFICATION

Is this your Social Security number?
Yes ◯   No ◯

④ TEST DATE

MM	D	D	Y	Y
Jan	0	0	200	0
Feb	1	1	200	1
Mar	2	2	200	2
Apr	3	3	200	3
May		4	200	4
Jun		5	200	5
Jul		6	200	6
Aug		7	200	7
Sep		8	200	8
Oct		9	200	9
Nov				
Dec				

⑤ CLASS NUMBER

⑥ RAW SCORE

Life Skills and Test Prep 3
Unit 6 Test Answer Sheet

① _____
  Last Name   First Name   Middle

② _____
  Teacher's Name

TEST

1 Ⓐ Ⓑ Ⓒ Ⓓ
2 Ⓐ Ⓑ Ⓒ Ⓓ
3 Ⓐ Ⓑ Ⓒ Ⓓ
4 Ⓐ Ⓑ Ⓒ Ⓓ
5 Ⓐ Ⓑ Ⓒ Ⓓ
6 Ⓐ Ⓑ Ⓒ Ⓓ
7 Ⓐ Ⓑ Ⓒ Ⓓ
8 Ⓐ Ⓑ Ⓒ Ⓓ
9 Ⓐ Ⓑ Ⓒ Ⓓ
10 Ⓐ Ⓑ Ⓒ Ⓓ
11 Ⓐ Ⓑ Ⓒ Ⓓ
12 Ⓐ Ⓑ Ⓒ Ⓓ
13 Ⓐ Ⓑ Ⓒ Ⓓ
14 Ⓐ Ⓑ Ⓒ Ⓓ
15 Ⓐ Ⓑ Ⓒ Ⓓ
16 Ⓐ Ⓑ Ⓒ Ⓓ
17 Ⓐ Ⓑ Ⓒ Ⓓ
18 Ⓐ Ⓑ Ⓒ Ⓓ
19 Ⓐ Ⓑ Ⓒ Ⓓ
20 Ⓐ Ⓑ Ⓒ Ⓓ

Directions for marking answers

- Use a No. 2 pencil. Do NOT use ink.
- Make dark marks and bubble in your answers completely.
- If you change an answer, erase your first mark completely.

Right
Ⓐ Ⓑ Ⓒ Ⓓ

Wrong
Ⓐ ⓧ Ⓒ Ⓓ
Ⓐ Ⓑ Ⓒ Ⓓ

③ **STUDENT IDENTIFICATION**

Is this your Social Security number?
Yes ☐   No ☐

④ **TEST DATE**

MM	D	D	Y	Y
Jan	0	0	200	0
Feb	1	1	200	1
Mar	2	2	200	2
Apr	3	3	200	3
May		4	200	4
Jun		5	200	5
Jul		6	200	6
Aug		7	200	7
Sep		8	200	8
Oct		9	200	9
Nov				
Dec				

⑤ **CLASS NUMBER**

⑥ **RAW SCORE**

Life Skills and Test Prep 3
Unit 6 Test Answer Sheet

① _____

    Last Name   First Name   Middle

② _____

    Teacher's Name

TEST

1 (A) (B) (C) (D)
2 (A) (B) (C) (D)
3 (A) (B) (C) (D)
4 (A) (B) (C) (D)
5 (A) (B) (C) (D)
6 (A) (B) (C) (D)
7 (A) (B) (C) (D)
8 (A) (B) (C) (D)
9 (A) (B) (C) (D)
10 (A) (B) (C) (D)
11 (A) (B) (C) (D)
12 (A) (B) (C) (D)
13 (A) (B) (C) (D)
14 (A) (B) (C) (D)
15 (A) (B) (C) (D)
16 (A) (B) (C) (D)
17 (A) (B) (C) (D)
18 (A) (B) (C) (D)
19 (A) (B) (C) (D)
20 (A) (B) (C) (D)

Directions for marking answers

- Use a No. 2 pencil. Do NOT use ink.
- Make dark marks and bubble in your answers completely.
- If you change an answer, erase your first mark completely.

Right
(A) (B) (C) (D)

Wrong
(A) (X) (C) (D)
(A) (B) (C) (D)

③ STUDENT IDENTIFICATION

0	0	0	0	0	0	0	0
1	1	1	1	1	1	1	1
2	2	2	2	2	2	2	2
3	3	3	3	3	3	3	3
4	4	4	4	4	4	4	4
5	5	5	5	5	5	5	5
6	6	6	6	6	6	6	6
7	7	7	7	7	7	7	7
8	8	8	8	8	8	8	8
9	9	9	9	9	9	9	9

Is this your Social Security number?
Yes ◯   No ◯

④ TEST DATE

MM	D	D	Y	Y
Jan ◯	0	0	200	0
Feb ◯	1	1	200	1
Mar ◯	2	2	200	2
Apr ◯	3	3	200	3
May ◯		4	200	4
Jun ◯		5	200	5
Jul ◯		6	200	6
Aug ◯		7	200	7
Sep ◯		8	200	8
Oct ◯		9	200	9
Nov ◯				
Dec ◯				

⑤ CLASS NUMBER

0	0	0	0	0	0	0	0
1	1	1	1	1	1	1	1
2	2	2	2	2	2	2	2
3	3	3	3	3	3	3	3
4	4	4	4	4	4	4	4
5	5	5	5	5	5	5	5
6	6	6	6	6	6	6	6
7	7	7	7	7	7	7	7
8	8	8	8	8	8	8	8
9	9	9	9	9	9	9	9

⑥ RAW SCORE

0	0
1	1
2	2
3	3
4	4
5	5
6	6
7	7
8	8
9	9

Life Skills and Test Prep 3
Unit 7 Test Answer Sheet

1) _____
   Last Name   First Name   Middle

2) _____
   Teacher's Name

TEST

1 Ⓐ Ⓑ Ⓒ Ⓓ
2 Ⓐ Ⓑ Ⓒ Ⓓ
3 Ⓐ Ⓑ Ⓒ Ⓓ
4 Ⓐ Ⓑ Ⓒ Ⓓ
5 Ⓐ Ⓑ Ⓒ Ⓓ
6 Ⓐ Ⓑ Ⓒ Ⓓ
7 Ⓐ Ⓑ Ⓒ Ⓓ
8 Ⓐ Ⓑ Ⓒ Ⓓ
9 Ⓐ Ⓑ Ⓒ Ⓓ
10 Ⓐ Ⓑ Ⓒ Ⓓ
11 Ⓐ Ⓑ Ⓒ Ⓓ
12 Ⓐ Ⓑ Ⓒ Ⓓ
13 Ⓐ Ⓑ Ⓒ Ⓓ
14 Ⓐ Ⓑ Ⓒ Ⓓ
15 Ⓐ Ⓑ Ⓒ Ⓓ
16 Ⓐ Ⓑ Ⓒ Ⓓ
17 Ⓐ Ⓑ Ⓒ Ⓓ
18 Ⓐ Ⓑ Ⓒ Ⓓ
19 Ⓐ Ⓑ Ⓒ Ⓓ
20 Ⓐ Ⓑ Ⓒ Ⓓ

Directions for marking answers

- Use a No. 2 pencil. Do NOT use ink.
- Make dark marks and bubble in your answers completely.
- If you change an answer, erase your first mark completely.

Right
Ⓐ ⬤ Ⓒ Ⓓ
Wrong
Ⓐ ⊗ Ⓒ Ⓓ
Ⓐ Ⓑ Ⓒ Ⓓ

③ **STUDENT IDENTIFICATION**

0 0 0   0 0   0 0 0 0
1 1 1   1 1   1 1 1 1
2 2 2   2 2   2 2 2 2
3 3 3   3 3   3 3 3 3
4 4 4   4 4   4 4 4 4
5 5 5   5 5   5 5 5 5
6 6 6   6 6   6 6 6 6
7 7 7   7 7   7 7 7 7
8 8 8   8 8   8 8 8 8
9 9 9   9 9   9 9 9 9

Is this your Social Security number?
Yes ◯ No ◯

④ **TEST DATE**

MM	D	D	Y	Y
Jan	0	0	200	0
Feb	1	1	200	1
Mar	2	2	200	2
Apr	3	3	200	3
May		4	200	4
Jun		5	200	5
Jul		6	200	6
Aug		7	200	7
Sep		8	200	8
Oct		9	200	9
Nov				
Dec				

⑤ **CLASS NUMBER**

0 0 0 0 0 0 0 0
1 1 1 1 1 1 1 1
2 2 2 2 2 2 2 2
3 3 3 3 3 3 3 3
4 4 4 4 4 4 4 4
5 5 5 5 5 5 5 5
6 6 6 6 6 6 6 6
7 7 7 7 7 7 7 7
8 8 8 8 8 8 8 8
9 9 9 9 9 9 9 9

⑥ **RAW SCORE**

0 0
1 1
2 2
3 3
4 4
5 5
6 6
7 7
8 8
9 9

Life Skills and Test Prep 3
Unit 7 Test Answer Sheet

① _____
Last Name   First Name   Middle

② _____
Teacher's Name

TEST

1 Ⓐ Ⓑ Ⓒ Ⓓ
2 Ⓐ Ⓑ Ⓒ Ⓓ
3 Ⓐ Ⓑ Ⓒ Ⓓ
4 Ⓐ Ⓑ Ⓒ Ⓓ
5 Ⓐ Ⓑ Ⓒ Ⓓ
6 Ⓐ Ⓑ Ⓒ Ⓓ
7 Ⓐ Ⓑ Ⓒ Ⓓ
8 Ⓐ Ⓑ Ⓒ Ⓓ
9 Ⓐ Ⓑ Ⓒ Ⓓ
10 Ⓐ Ⓑ Ⓒ Ⓓ
11 Ⓐ Ⓑ Ⓒ Ⓓ
12 Ⓐ Ⓑ Ⓒ Ⓓ
13 Ⓐ Ⓑ Ⓒ Ⓓ
14 Ⓐ Ⓑ Ⓒ Ⓓ
15 Ⓐ Ⓑ Ⓒ Ⓓ
16 Ⓐ Ⓑ Ⓒ Ⓓ
17 Ⓐ Ⓑ Ⓒ Ⓓ
18 Ⓐ Ⓑ Ⓒ Ⓓ
19 Ⓐ Ⓑ Ⓒ Ⓓ
20 Ⓐ Ⓑ Ⓒ Ⓓ

Directions for marking answers

- Use a No. 2 pencil. Do NOT use ink.
- Make dark marks and bubble in your answers completely.
- If you change an answer, erase your first mark completely.

Right
Ⓐ Ⓑ Ⓒ Ⓓ

Wrong
Ⓐ Ⓧ Ⓒ Ⓓ
Ⓐ Ⓑ Ⓒ Ⓓ

③ **STUDENT IDENTIFICATION**

Is this your Social Security number?
Yes ⃝ No ⃝

④ **TEST DATE**

MM	D	D	Y	Y
Jan	0	0	200	0
Feb	1	1	200	1
Mar	2	2	200	2
Apr	3	3	200	3
May		4	200	4
Jun		5	200	5
Jul		6	200	6
Aug		7	200	7
Sep		8	200	8
Oct		9	200	9
Nov				
Dec				

⑤ **CLASS NUMBER**

⑥ **RAW SCORE**

① _____

    Last Name   First Name   Middle

② _____

    Teacher's Name

TEST

1 Ⓐ Ⓑ Ⓒ Ⓓ
2 Ⓐ Ⓑ Ⓒ Ⓓ
3 Ⓐ Ⓑ Ⓒ Ⓓ
4 Ⓐ Ⓑ Ⓒ Ⓓ
5 Ⓐ Ⓑ Ⓒ Ⓓ
6 Ⓐ Ⓑ Ⓒ Ⓓ
7 Ⓐ Ⓑ Ⓒ Ⓓ
8 Ⓐ Ⓑ Ⓒ Ⓓ
9 Ⓐ Ⓑ Ⓒ Ⓓ
10 Ⓐ Ⓑ Ⓒ Ⓓ
11 Ⓐ Ⓑ Ⓒ Ⓓ
12 Ⓐ Ⓑ Ⓒ Ⓓ
13 Ⓐ Ⓑ Ⓒ Ⓓ
14 Ⓐ Ⓑ Ⓒ Ⓓ
15 Ⓐ Ⓑ Ⓒ Ⓓ
16 Ⓐ Ⓑ Ⓒ Ⓓ
17 Ⓐ Ⓑ Ⓒ Ⓓ
18 Ⓐ Ⓑ Ⓒ Ⓓ
19 Ⓐ Ⓑ Ⓒ Ⓓ
20 Ⓐ Ⓑ Ⓒ Ⓓ

Directions for marking answers

- Use a No. 2 pencil. Do NOT use ink.
- Make dark marks and bubble in your answers completely.
- If you change an answer, erase your first mark completely.

Right
Ⓐ ⬤B Ⓒ Ⓓ

Wrong
Ⓐ ⊗ Ⓒ Ⓓ
Ⓐ Ⓑ Ⓒ Ⓓ

③ **STUDENT IDENTIFICATION**

Is this your Social Security number?
Yes ⬭ No ⬭

④ **TEST DATE**

MM	D	D	Y	Y
Jan	⓪	⓪	200	⓪
Feb	①	①	200	①
Mar	②	②	200	②
Apr	③	③	200	③
May		④	200	④
Jun		⑤	200	⑤
Jul		⑥	200	⑥
Aug		⑦	200	⑦
Sep		⑧	200	⑧
Oct		⑨	200	⑨
Nov				
Dec				

⑤ **CLASS NUMBER**

⑥ **RAW SCORE**

① _____
  Last Name   First Name   Middle

② _____
  Teacher's Name

TEST

1 Ⓐ Ⓑ Ⓒ Ⓓ
2 Ⓐ Ⓑ Ⓒ Ⓓ
3 Ⓐ Ⓑ Ⓒ Ⓓ
4 Ⓐ Ⓑ Ⓒ Ⓓ
5 Ⓐ Ⓑ Ⓒ Ⓓ
6 Ⓐ Ⓑ Ⓒ Ⓓ
7 Ⓐ Ⓑ Ⓒ Ⓓ
8 Ⓐ Ⓑ Ⓒ Ⓓ
9 Ⓐ Ⓑ Ⓒ Ⓓ
10 Ⓐ Ⓑ Ⓒ Ⓓ
11 Ⓐ Ⓑ Ⓒ Ⓓ
12 Ⓐ Ⓑ Ⓒ Ⓓ
13 Ⓐ Ⓑ Ⓒ Ⓓ
14 Ⓐ Ⓑ Ⓒ Ⓓ
15 Ⓐ Ⓑ Ⓒ Ⓓ
16 Ⓐ Ⓑ Ⓒ Ⓓ
17 Ⓐ Ⓑ Ⓒ Ⓓ
18 Ⓐ Ⓑ Ⓒ Ⓓ
19 Ⓐ Ⓑ Ⓒ Ⓓ
20 Ⓐ Ⓑ Ⓒ Ⓓ

Directions for marking answers

- Use a No. 2 pencil. Do NOT use ink.
- Make dark marks and bubble in your answers completely.
- If you change an answer, erase your first mark completely.

Right
Ⓐ Ⓑ Ⓒ Ⓓ

Wrong
Ⓐ Ⓑ Ⓒ Ⓓ
Ⓐ Ⓑ Ⓒ Ⓓ

③ **STUDENT IDENTIFICATION**

Is this your Social Security number?
Yes ◯   No ◯

④ **TEST DATE**

MM	D	D	Y	Y
Jan	0	0	200	0
Feb	1	1	200	1
Mar	2	2	200	2
Apr	3	3	200	3
May		4	200	4
Jun		5	200	5
Jul		6	200	6
Aug		7	200	7
Sep		8	200	8
Oct		9	200	9
Nov				
Dec				

⑤ **CLASS NUMBER**

⑥ **RAW SCORE**

Life Skills and Test Prep 3
Unit 9 Test Answer Sheet

① _____

　　Last Name　　　　　　First Name　　　　　Middle

② _____

　　Teacher's Name

TEST

1　Ⓐ Ⓑ Ⓒ Ⓓ
2　Ⓐ Ⓑ Ⓒ Ⓓ
3　Ⓐ Ⓑ Ⓒ Ⓓ
4　Ⓐ Ⓑ Ⓒ Ⓓ
5　Ⓐ Ⓑ Ⓒ Ⓓ
6　Ⓐ Ⓑ Ⓒ Ⓓ
7　Ⓐ Ⓑ Ⓒ Ⓓ
8　Ⓐ Ⓑ Ⓒ Ⓓ
9　Ⓐ Ⓑ Ⓒ Ⓓ
10　Ⓐ Ⓑ Ⓒ Ⓓ
11　Ⓐ Ⓑ Ⓒ Ⓓ
12　Ⓐ Ⓑ Ⓒ Ⓓ
13　Ⓐ Ⓑ Ⓒ Ⓓ
14　Ⓐ Ⓑ Ⓒ Ⓓ
15　Ⓐ Ⓑ Ⓒ Ⓓ
16　Ⓐ Ⓑ Ⓒ Ⓓ
17　Ⓐ Ⓑ Ⓒ Ⓓ
18　Ⓐ Ⓑ Ⓒ Ⓓ
19　Ⓐ Ⓑ Ⓒ Ⓓ
20　Ⓐ Ⓑ Ⓒ Ⓓ

Directions for marking answers

- Use a No. 2 pencil. Do NOT use ink.
- Make dark marks and bubble in your answers completely.
- If you change an answer, erase your first mark completely.

Right
Ⓐ Ⓑ Ⓒ Ⓓ

Wrong
Ⓐ Ⓧ Ⓒ Ⓓ
Ⓐ Ⓑ Ⓒ Ⓓ

③ **STUDENT IDENTIFICATION**

0 0 0 0 0 0 0 0
1 1 1 1 1 1 1 1
2 2 2 2 2 2 2 2
3 3 3 3 3 3 3 3
4 4 4 4 4 4 4 4
5 5 5 5 5 5 5 5
6 6 6 6 6 6 6 6
7 7 7 7 7 7 7 7
8 8 8 8 8 8 8 8
9 9 9 9 9 9 9 9

Is this your Social Security number?
Yes ◯　No ◯

④ **TEST DATE**

MM	D	D	Y	Y
Jan	0	0	200	0
Feb	1	1	200	1
Mar	2	2	200	2
Apr	3	3	200	3
May		4	200	4
Jun		5	200	5
Jul		6	200	6
Aug		7	200	7
Sep		8	200	8
Oct		9	200	9
Nov				
Dec				

⑤ **CLASS NUMBER**

0 0 0 0 0 0 0 0
1 1 1 1 1 1 1 1
2 2 2 2 2 2 2 2
3 3 3 3 3 3 3 3
4 4 4 4 4 4 4 4
5 5 5 5 5 5 5 5
6 6 6 6 6 6 6 6
7 7 7 7 7 7 7 7
8 8 8 8 8 8 8 8
9 9 9 9 9 9 9 9

⑥ **RAW SCORE**

0 0
1 1
2 2
3 3
4 4
5 5
6 6
7 7
8 8
9 9

① _____
Last Name　　　　　　First Name　　　　　Middle

② _____
Teacher's Name

TEST

1 Ⓐ Ⓑ Ⓒ Ⓓ
2 Ⓐ Ⓑ Ⓒ Ⓓ
3 Ⓐ Ⓑ Ⓒ Ⓓ
4 Ⓐ Ⓑ Ⓒ Ⓓ
5 Ⓐ Ⓑ Ⓒ Ⓓ
6 Ⓐ Ⓑ Ⓒ Ⓓ
7 Ⓐ Ⓑ Ⓒ Ⓓ
8 Ⓐ Ⓑ Ⓒ Ⓓ
9 Ⓐ Ⓑ Ⓒ Ⓓ
10 Ⓐ Ⓑ Ⓒ Ⓓ
11 Ⓐ Ⓑ Ⓒ Ⓓ
12 Ⓐ Ⓑ Ⓒ Ⓓ
13 Ⓐ Ⓑ Ⓒ Ⓓ
14 Ⓐ Ⓑ Ⓒ Ⓓ
15 Ⓐ Ⓑ Ⓒ Ⓓ
16 Ⓐ Ⓑ Ⓒ Ⓓ
17 Ⓐ Ⓑ Ⓒ Ⓓ
18 Ⓐ Ⓑ Ⓒ Ⓓ
19 Ⓐ Ⓑ Ⓒ Ⓓ
20 Ⓐ Ⓑ Ⓒ Ⓓ

Directions for marking answers

- Use a No. 2 pencil. Do NOT use ink.
- Make dark marks and bubble in your answers completely.
- If you change an answer, erase your first mark completely.

Right
Ⓐ ■Ⓑ Ⓒ Ⓓ

Wrong
Ⓐ ⊗ Ⓒ Ⓓ
Ⓐ Ⓑ Ⓒ Ⓓ

③ STUDENT IDENTIFICATION

0	0	0	0	0	0	0	0	0
1	1	1	1	1	1	1	1	1
2	2	2	2	2	2	2	2	2
3	3	3	3	3	3	3	3	3
4	4	4	4	4	4	4	4	4
5	5	5	5	5	5	5	5	5
6	6	6	6	6	6	6	6	6
7	7	7	7	7	7	7	7	7
8	8	8	8	8	8	8	8	8
9	9	9	9	9	9	9	9	9

Is this your Social Security number?
Yes ◯　No ◯

④ TEST DATE

MM	D	D	Y	Y
Jan ◯	0	0	200	0
Feb ◯	1	1	200	1
Mar ◯	2	2	200	2
Apr ◯	3	3	200	3
May ◯		4	200	4
Jun ◯		5	200	5
Jul ◯		6	200	6
Aug ◯		7	200	7
Sep ◯		8	200	8
Oct ◯		9	200	9
Nov ◯				
Dec ◯				

⑤ CLASS NUMBER

0	0	0	0	0	0	0	0
1	1	1	1	1	1	1	1
2	2	2	2	2	2	2	2
3	3	3	3	3	3	3	3
4	4	4	4	4	4	4	4
5	5	5	5	5	5	5	5
6	6	6	6	6	6	6	6
7	7	7	7	7	7	7	7
8	8	8	8	8	8	8	8
9	9	9	9	9	9	9	9

⑥ RAW SCORE

0	0
1	1
2	2
3	3
4	4
5	5
6	6
7	7
8	8
9	9

Life Skills and Test Prep 3
Unit 10 Test Answer Sheet

① _____

    Last Name   First Name   Middle

② _____

    Teacher's Name

TEST

1 (A) (B) (C) (D)
2 (A) (B) (C) (D)
3 (A) (B) (C) (D)
4 (A) (B) (C) (D)
5 (A) (B) (C) (D)
6 (A) (B) (C) (D)
7 (A) (B) (C) (D)
8 (A) (B) (C) (D)
9 (A) (B) (C) (D)
10 (A) (B) (C) (D)
11 (A) (B) (C) (D)
12 (A) (B) (C) (D)
13 (A) (B) (C) (D)
14 (A) (B) (C) (D)
15 (A) (B) (C) (D)
16 (A) (B) (C) (D)
17 (A) (B) (C) (D)
18 (A) (B) (C) (D)
19 (A) (B) (C) (D)
20 (A) (B) (C) (D)

Directions for marking answers

- Use a No. 2 pencil. Do NOT use ink.
- Make dark marks and bubble in your answers completely.
- If you change an answer, erase your first mark completely.

Right
(A) (B) (C) (D)

Wrong
(A) (X) (C) (D)
(A) (B) (C) (D)

③ **STUDENT IDENTIFICATION**

0	0	0	0	0	0	0	0	0
1	1	1	1	1	1	1	1	1
2	2	2	2	2	2	2	2	2
3	3	3	3	3	3	3	3	3
4	4	4	4	4	4	4	4	4
5	5	5	5	5	5	5	5	5
6	6	6	6	6	6	6	6	6
7	7	7	7	7	7	7	7	7
8	8	8	8	8	8	8	8	8
9	9	9	9	9	9	9	9	9

Is this your Social Security number?
Yes ◯   No ◯

④ **TEST DATE**

MM	D	D	Y	Y
Jan ◯	0	0	200	0
Feb ◯	1	1	200	1
Mar ◯	2	2	200	2
Apr ◯	3	3	200	3
May ◯		4	200	4
Jun ◯		5	200	5
Jul ◯		6	200	6
Aug ◯		7	200	7
Sep ◯		8	200	8
Oct ◯		9	200	9
Nov ◯				
Dec ◯				

⑤ **CLASS NUMBER**

0	0	0	0	0	0	0	0
1	1	1	1	1	1	1	1
2	2	2	2	2	2	2	2
3	3	3	3	3	3	3	3
4	4	4	4	4	4	4	4
5	5	5	5	5	5	5	5
6	6	6	6	6	6	6	6
7	7	7	7	7	7	7	7
8	8	8	8	8	8	8	8
9	9	9	9	9	9	9	9

⑥ **RAW SCORE**

0	0
1	1
2	2
3	3
4	4
5	5
6	6
7	7
8	8
9	9

Life Skills and Test Prep 3
Unit 10 Test Answer Sheet

① _____

Last Name   First Name   Middle

② _____

Teacher's Name

TEST

1 Ⓐ Ⓑ Ⓒ Ⓓ
2 Ⓐ Ⓑ Ⓒ Ⓓ
3 Ⓐ Ⓑ Ⓒ Ⓓ
4 Ⓐ Ⓑ Ⓒ Ⓓ
5 Ⓐ Ⓑ Ⓒ Ⓓ
6 Ⓐ Ⓑ Ⓒ Ⓓ
7 Ⓐ Ⓑ Ⓒ Ⓓ
8 Ⓐ Ⓑ Ⓒ Ⓓ
9 Ⓐ Ⓑ Ⓒ Ⓓ
10 Ⓐ Ⓑ Ⓒ Ⓓ
11 Ⓐ Ⓑ Ⓒ Ⓓ
12 Ⓐ Ⓑ Ⓒ Ⓓ
13 Ⓐ Ⓑ Ⓒ Ⓓ
14 Ⓐ Ⓑ Ⓒ Ⓓ
15 Ⓐ Ⓑ Ⓒ Ⓓ
16 Ⓐ Ⓑ Ⓒ Ⓓ
17 Ⓐ Ⓑ Ⓒ Ⓓ
18 Ⓐ Ⓑ Ⓒ Ⓓ
19 Ⓐ Ⓑ Ⓒ Ⓓ
20 Ⓐ Ⓑ Ⓒ Ⓓ

Directions for marking answers

- Use a No. 2 pencil. Do NOT use ink.
- Make dark marks and bubble in your answers completely.
- If you change an answer, erase your first mark completely.

Right

Ⓐ ⬤Ⓑ Ⓒ Ⓓ

Wrong

Ⓐ ⓧ Ⓒ Ⓓ
Ⓐ Ⓑ Ⓒ Ⓓ

③ **STUDENT IDENTIFICATION**

⓪	⓪	⓪	⓪	⓪	⓪	⓪	⓪	⓪
①	①	①	①	①	①	①	①	①
②	②	②	②	②	②	②	②	②
③	③	③	③	③	③	③	③	③
④	④	④	④	④	④	④	④	④
⑤	⑤	⑤	⑤	⑤	⑤	⑤	⑤	⑤
⑥	⑥	⑥	⑥	⑥	⑥	⑥	⑥	⑥
⑦	⑦	⑦	⑦	⑦	⑦	⑦	⑦	⑦
⑧	⑧	⑧	⑧	⑧	⑧	⑧	⑧	⑧
⑨	⑨	⑨	⑨	⑨	⑨	⑨	⑨	⑨

Is this your Social Security number?
Yes ◯   No ◯

④ **TEST DATE**

MM	D	D	Y	Y
Jan ◯	⓪	⓪	200	⓪
Feb ◯	①	①	200	①
Mar ◯	②	②	200	②
Apr ◯	③	③	200	③
May ◯		④	200	④
Jun ◯		⑤	200	⑤
Jul ◯		⑥	200	⑥
Aug ◯		⑦	200	⑦
Sep ◯		⑧	200	⑧
Oct ◯		⑨	200	⑨
Nov ◯				
Dec ◯				

⑤ **CLASS NUMBER**

⓪	⓪	⓪	⓪	⓪	⓪	⓪	⓪
①	①	①	①	①	①	①	①
②	②	②	②	②	②	②	②
③	③	③	③	③	③	③	③
④	④	④	④	④	④	④	④
⑤	⑤	⑤	⑤	⑤	⑤	⑤	⑤
⑥	⑥	⑥	⑥	⑥	⑥	⑥	⑥
⑦	⑦	⑦	⑦	⑦	⑦	⑦	⑦
⑧	⑧	⑧	⑧	⑧	⑧	⑧	⑧
⑨	⑨	⑨	⑨	⑨	⑨	⑨	⑨

⑥ **RAW SCORE**

⓪	⓪
①	①
②	②
③	③
④	④
⑤	⑤
⑥	⑥
⑦	⑦
⑧	⑧
⑨	⑨

Life Skills and Test Prep 3
Unit 11 Test Answer Sheet

① _____
    Last Name   First Name   Middle

② _____
    Teacher's Name

TEST

1 Ⓐ Ⓑ Ⓒ Ⓓ
2 Ⓐ Ⓑ Ⓒ Ⓓ
3 Ⓐ Ⓑ Ⓒ Ⓓ
4 Ⓐ Ⓑ Ⓒ Ⓓ
5 Ⓐ Ⓑ Ⓒ Ⓓ
6 Ⓐ Ⓑ Ⓒ Ⓓ
7 Ⓐ Ⓑ Ⓒ Ⓓ
8 Ⓐ Ⓑ Ⓒ Ⓓ
9 Ⓐ Ⓑ Ⓒ Ⓓ
10 Ⓐ Ⓑ Ⓒ Ⓓ
11 Ⓐ Ⓑ Ⓒ Ⓓ
12 Ⓐ Ⓑ Ⓒ Ⓓ
13 Ⓐ Ⓑ Ⓒ Ⓓ
14 Ⓐ Ⓑ Ⓒ Ⓓ
15 Ⓐ Ⓑ Ⓒ Ⓓ
16 Ⓐ Ⓑ Ⓒ Ⓓ
17 Ⓐ Ⓑ Ⓒ Ⓓ
18 Ⓐ Ⓑ Ⓒ Ⓓ
19 Ⓐ Ⓑ Ⓒ Ⓓ
20 Ⓐ Ⓑ Ⓒ Ⓓ

Directions for marking answers

- Use a No. 2 pencil. Do NOT use ink.
- Make dark marks and bubble in your answers completely.
- If you change an answer, erase your first mark completely.

Right
Ⓐ Ⓑ Ⓒ Ⓓ
Wrong
Ⓐ Ⓧ Ⓒ Ⓓ
Ⓐ Ⓑ Ⓒ Ⓓ

③ STUDENT IDENTIFICATION

(grid of bubbles 0–9)

Is this your Social Security number?
Yes ◯ No ◯

④ TEST DATE

MM	D	D	Y	Y
Jan	⓪	⓪	200	⓪
Feb	①	①	200	①
Mar	②	②	200	②
Apr	③	③	200	③
May		④	200	④
Jun		⑤	200	⑤
Jul		⑥	200	⑥
Aug		⑦	200	⑦
Sep		⑧	200	⑧
Oct		⑨	200	⑨
Nov				
Dec				

⑤ CLASS NUMBER

(grid of bubbles 0–9)

⑥ RAW SCORE

(grid of bubbles 0–9)

Life Skills and Test Prep 3
Unit 11 Test Answer Sheet

① _____
　Last Name　　　　First Name　　　　Middle

② _____
　Teacher's Name

TEST

1 Ⓐ Ⓑ Ⓒ Ⓓ
2 Ⓐ Ⓑ Ⓒ Ⓓ
3 Ⓐ Ⓑ Ⓒ Ⓓ
4 Ⓐ Ⓑ Ⓒ Ⓓ
5 Ⓐ Ⓑ Ⓒ Ⓓ
6 Ⓐ Ⓑ Ⓒ Ⓓ
7 Ⓐ Ⓑ Ⓒ Ⓓ
8 Ⓐ Ⓑ Ⓒ Ⓓ
9 Ⓐ Ⓑ Ⓒ Ⓓ
10 Ⓐ Ⓑ Ⓒ Ⓓ
11 Ⓐ Ⓑ Ⓒ Ⓓ
12 Ⓐ Ⓑ Ⓒ Ⓓ
13 Ⓐ Ⓑ Ⓒ Ⓓ
14 Ⓐ Ⓑ Ⓒ Ⓓ
15 Ⓐ Ⓑ Ⓒ Ⓓ
16 Ⓐ Ⓑ Ⓒ Ⓓ
17 Ⓐ Ⓑ Ⓒ Ⓓ
18 Ⓐ Ⓑ Ⓒ Ⓓ
19 Ⓐ Ⓑ Ⓒ Ⓓ
20 Ⓐ Ⓑ Ⓒ Ⓓ

Directions for marking answers

- Use a No. 2 pencil. Do NOT use ink.
- Make dark marks and bubble in your answers completely.
- If you change an answer, erase your first mark completely.

Right
Ⓐ ⬛Ⓑ Ⓒ Ⓓ

Wrong
Ⓐ ⓧ Ⓒ Ⓓ
Ⓐ ⓑ Ⓒ Ⓓ

③ STUDENT IDENTIFICATION

Is this your Social Security number?
Yes ◯　No ◯

④ TEST DATE

MM	D	D	Y	Y
Jan ◯	0	0	200	0
Feb ◯	1	1	200	1
Mar ◯	2	2	200	2
Apr ◯	3	3	200	3
May ◯		4	200	4
Jun ◯		5	200	5
Jul ◯		6	200	6
Aug ◯		7	200	7
Sep ◯		8	200	8
Oct ◯		9	200	9
Nov ◯				
Dec ◯				

⑤ CLASS NUMBER

⑥ RAW SCORE

Life Skills and Test Prep 3
Unit 12 Test Answer Sheet

① _____

    Last Name   First Name   Middle

② _____

    Teacher's Name

TEST

1 Ⓐ Ⓑ Ⓒ Ⓓ
2 Ⓐ Ⓑ Ⓒ Ⓓ
3 Ⓐ Ⓑ Ⓒ Ⓓ
4 Ⓐ Ⓑ Ⓒ Ⓓ
5 Ⓐ Ⓑ Ⓒ Ⓓ
6 Ⓐ Ⓑ Ⓒ Ⓓ
7 Ⓐ Ⓑ Ⓒ Ⓓ
8 Ⓐ Ⓑ Ⓒ Ⓓ
9 Ⓐ Ⓑ Ⓒ Ⓓ
10 Ⓐ Ⓑ Ⓒ Ⓓ
11 Ⓐ Ⓑ Ⓒ Ⓓ
12 Ⓐ Ⓑ Ⓒ Ⓓ
13 Ⓐ Ⓑ Ⓒ Ⓓ
14 Ⓐ Ⓑ Ⓒ Ⓓ
15 Ⓐ Ⓑ Ⓒ Ⓓ
16 Ⓐ Ⓑ Ⓒ Ⓓ
17 Ⓐ Ⓑ Ⓒ Ⓓ
18 Ⓐ Ⓑ Ⓒ Ⓓ
19 Ⓐ Ⓑ Ⓒ Ⓓ
20 Ⓐ Ⓑ Ⓒ Ⓓ

Directions for marking answers

- Use a No. 2 pencil. Do NOT use ink.
- Make dark marks and bubble in your answers completely.
- If you change an answer, erase your first mark completely.

Right
Ⓐ ● Ⓒ Ⓓ

Wrong
Ⓐ ⊗ Ⓒ Ⓓ
Ⓐ Ⓑ Ⓒ Ⓓ

③ STUDENT IDENTIFICATION

Is this your Social Security number?
Yes ◯ No ◯

④ TEST DATE

Jan ◯ Feb ◯ Mar ◯ Apr ◯ May ◯ Jun ◯ Jul ◯ Aug ◯ Sep ◯ Oct ◯ Nov ◯ Dec ◯

⑤ CLASS NUMBER

⑥ RAW SCORE

Life Skills and Test Prep 3
Unit 12 Test Answer Sheet

① _____

Last Name   First Name   Middle

② _____

Teacher's Name

TEST

1 Ⓐ Ⓑ Ⓒ Ⓓ
2 Ⓐ Ⓑ Ⓒ Ⓓ
3 Ⓐ Ⓑ Ⓒ Ⓓ
4 Ⓐ Ⓑ Ⓒ Ⓓ
5 Ⓐ Ⓑ Ⓒ Ⓓ
6 Ⓐ Ⓑ Ⓒ Ⓓ
7 Ⓐ Ⓑ Ⓒ Ⓓ
8 Ⓐ Ⓑ Ⓒ Ⓓ
9 Ⓐ Ⓑ Ⓒ Ⓓ
10 Ⓐ Ⓑ Ⓒ Ⓓ
11 Ⓐ Ⓑ Ⓒ Ⓓ
12 Ⓐ Ⓑ Ⓒ Ⓓ
13 Ⓐ Ⓑ Ⓒ Ⓓ
14 Ⓐ Ⓑ Ⓒ Ⓓ
15 Ⓐ Ⓑ Ⓒ Ⓓ
16 Ⓐ Ⓑ Ⓒ Ⓓ
17 Ⓐ Ⓑ Ⓒ Ⓓ
18 Ⓐ Ⓑ Ⓒ Ⓓ
19 Ⓐ Ⓑ Ⓒ Ⓓ
20 Ⓐ Ⓑ Ⓒ Ⓓ

Directions for marking answers

- Use a No. 2 pencil. Do NOT use ink.
- Make dark marks and bubble in your answers completely.
- If you change an answer, erase your first mark completely.

Right
Ⓐ ● Ⓒ Ⓓ

Wrong
Ⓐ ⊗ Ⓒ Ⓓ
Ⓐ Ⓑ Ⓒ Ⓓ

③ **STUDENT IDENTIFICATION**

Is this your Social Security number?
Yes ⃝   No ⃝

④ **TEST DATE**

MM	D	D	Y	Y
Jan	0	0	200	0
Feb	1	1	200	1
Mar	2	2	200	2
Apr	3	3	200	3
May		4	200	4
Jun		5	200	5
Jul		6	200	6
Aug		7	200	7
Sep		8	200	8
Oct		9	200	9
Nov				
Dec				

⑤ **CLASS NUMBER**

⑥ **RAW SCORE**